Selwyn Brinton

The renaissance in Italian art: Sculpture and painting

A handbook for students and travellers

Selwyn Brinton

The renaissance in Italian art: Sculpture and painting
A handbook for students and travellers

ISBN/EAN: 9783337210755

Printed in Europe, USA, Canada, Australia, Japan

Cover: Foto ©Thomas Meinert / pixelio.de

More available books at **www.hansebooks.com**

PART I.

THE
RENAISSANCE IN ITALIAN ART
(Sculpture and Painting).

A HANDBOOK FOR STUDENTS AND TRAVELLERS.

IN THREE PARTS. EACH PART COMPLETE IN ITSELF.

ILLUSTRATED, AND WITH SEPARATE APPENDIX AND INDEX.

BY

SELWYN BRINTON, B.A.
(BARRISTER-AT-LAW).

LONDON:
SIMPKIN, MARSHALL, HAMILTON, KENT & Co., LIMITED.

1898.

PART I.

FLORENCE, PISA, SIENA.

PREFACE.

In considering the vast amount of literature which this fascinating subject of Italian Art has called forth, varying from the heaviest and most profound research to the most brilliant and most delicate criticism, he needs must be a bold spirit who would approach the venerated pile, even though he be armed at all points with the results of some intimate and detailed inquiry, some new theory on a debatable or neglected artist.

Yet even if unarmed with these latter weapons—defensive or offensive—it has appeared to the present writer that there was a really useful work here to be done ; and that this work lay as much in classifying and placing in a readable and popular form the knowledge which exists, as in adding to it by the results of fresh investigation. In his own case he had found that spaces of clear light, where some school or artist had engaged his special interest, were separated by interspaces of dim twilight or even total darkness ; and in the attempt to co-ordinate in a detailed form the whole extent of that marvellous chain of evolution, which we call Italian Art, he found an immense help, a far wider and truer outlook, even to his clearest knowledge. The result of this attempt he has, after careful consideration and revision, ventured to place before the public, in the belief that what he found beneficial to himself might perhaps be helpful to others.

With the increase of knowledge the number of those who in travel, and of those who, while remaining at home, acquire an interest in art increases every day ; yet among these how many will carry the voluminous and detailed works of Crowe and Cavalcaselle in their trunks, or even find time for the invaluable but highly technical criticisms of Morelli ?

They become interested in art, they gain a certain knowledge of certain favourite painters, and there their progress remains; it is to this class, so large and so constantly increasing, in England, on the Continent, and in America, that this work appeals, because it presents a detailed, and yet, it is believed, a clearly-written and interesting account of the Italian schools, studied from that standpoint of evolution, which alone affords a chain of continued interest. In a work of this nature, which is thus essentially popular in its aim, a difficulty occurs in this fact, that points of more purely technical criticism, such, for instance, as the much-debated Rafaelle sketch-book question (treated in Part III., Appendix) would affect the straightforward and simple character of the work, and yet in some cases can hardly be passed over. I have tried to meet this difficulty by treating them separately in the Appendix, which I will none the less commend to the reader's more careful interest. The work will consist of three parts, which will deal, speaking broadly, with the Florentine, Venetian, and Roman schools, though the lesser schools will find their place in the analysis.

Each part will be issued separately, illustrated, and with separate Appendix and separate Index; and it is hoped that the whole work, being well advanced, will be placed before the public at no great interval, including with the last volume a neat case, to hold the three complete parts, which it has been sought to keep both popular in price, and of a thoroughly handy and portable size.

This work is, therefore, by no means intended to supplement, but rather to lead up to the careful study of the existing text-books. It is proposed, for the benefit of the interested student, to enclose a list of works to be studied in the Appendix of Part III.; and, in the meantime, it is a privilege to the author to be able to acknowledge his obligations, amongst others, to such works as Messrs. Crowe and Cavalcaselle's "History of Painting in Italy," and "North Italy," of which Morelli himself spoke with commendation; as Symonds' profound and brilliant work on the Italian Renaissance—the study of a great scholar's lifetime ; as Cosmo Monkhouse's charming work, published only lately, on the National Gallery, to which may be added usefully Mr. Cook's Handbook on the same collection ; as Kugler's "Handbook of Painting," and Perkins' "Tuscan Sculptors," and the recent studies of Grant Allen, of Leader Scott, and Berensen, and that interesting work on "Die Kunst der Renaissance," published last year by Adolf Philippi ; and last, but not least, the late Signor Morelli's "Kunst Kritische studien über Italienische Malerei" (Munich, Dresden, Berlin (1893), and Italian galleries).

On the side, too, of illustrations, the author must acknowledge his obligations to the kindness more especially of Messrs. F. and O. Brockmann (Dresden), Franz Hanfstaengl (Munich, London, and New York), and that well-known photographer, Signore Salviati (Venice), from whose prints the illustrations have been reproduced with great care and attention by Messrs. Hanfstaengl.

In conclusion, it is hoped that, if this little work has been carefully carried through, it may find a welcome among all to whom this wonderful growth of Italian Art is a thing of sympathy and interest; and that not alone in England, but also in Italy, in France, in that Germany where, as Morelli said, art culture is a serious pursuit—"ein wahrhaft ernstes Studium"—in the ever growing and widening culture of our busy brothers across the Atlantic, and of those free communities which are springing up throughout the world under the English flag.

For the writer on Art, like the happy worker in Art, has surely this inestimable happiness and blessing, that he may look beyond the miserable antipathies and prejudices of classes or creeds or nations, that he speaks a language which is the common heritage of all mankind, of all the universe—the language of Beauty, which is a part of the eternal utterance of God.

LIST OF ILLUSTRATIONS

PART I

1. "THE VIRGIN AND CHILD WITH ANGELS IN
   SERVICE" . . . . *Frontispiece*
   By SANDRO BOTTICELLI (*Berlin Gallery*).

   PAGE
2. "S. CLARA AT THE DEATH OF S. FRANCIS" . 4
   By GIOTTO BONDONE (*S. Francesco of Assisi*).

3. "A WINDOW OF GIOTTO'S CAMPANILE" . . . 5
   By GIOTTO BONDONE (*Duomo of Florence*).

4. "PULPIT OF THE CATHEDRAL OF SIENA" . . . 8
   By NICCOLA PISANO (*Duomo of Siena*).

5. "DAVID VICTORIOUS OVER GOLIATH" . . . 30
   By DONATO DI BETTI BARDI (called DONATELLO)
   (*Bargello of Florence*).

6. "GATTAMELATA THE CONDOTTIERE" 31
   By DONATO DI BETTI BARDI (called DONATELLO)
   (*Before S. Antonio of Padua*).

7. "GROUP OF ANGELS" 35
   By AGOSTINO DI DUCCIO (*S. Bernardino of Perugia*).

8. "STATUE OF THE CONDOTTIERE COLLEONI" . . 46
   By ANDREA VEROCCHIO (completed by LEOPARDI)
   (*Venice*).

9. "THE BLESSED IN PARADISE" (*detail*) . . 53
   By FRA ANGELICO (*Academy of Florence*).

xiii

LIST OF ILLUSTRATIONS.

                                                              PAGE

10. "THE CORONATION OF THE VIRGIN" (*detail*) . . 58

     By FRA FILIPPO LIPPI (*Academy of Florence*).

11. "THE CORONATION OF THE VIRGIN" 66

     By SANDRO FILIPEPI (*called* BOTTICELLI) (*Uffizi Gallery, Florence*).

12. "THE BIRTH OF VENUS FROM THE WAVES" (*detail*). 70

     By SANDRO FILIPEPI (*called* BOTTICELLI) (*Uffizi Gallery, Florence*).

E RENAISSANCE IN ITALIAN ART
(Sculpture and Painting).

CHAPTER I.

THE AWAKENING OF LIFE.

) are to trace the first roots of the great Renaissance lian Art, our thoughts must obviously be carried back ;h the ages, till at length perchance they will rest—at s. Mr. Ruskin, in one of his writings, has claimed for schools alone the right of being schools of perfect art,)ols, that is, which did their work as well as it is sible to do it," these being the Athenian, the Florentine, enetian ; and it is this mighty tradition of the Hellenic upreme and glorious in the great days of Athens, still ant and revered during the Roman Empire, that we find last senility in these Byzantine paintings, in that era greca" where art had become a mechanism, where is all but extinct.

we would inquire further into the later steps of this), we shall find them preserved to us less in the fleeting ials of the Catacombs—the outcome of a period of ion and danger—than in the almost eternal work of saicist. These sacred figures of Christ and Madonna, apostles, confessors, and martyrs of Rome (S. Puden- S. Teodoro, S. Lorenzo fuori le mura), of Byzantium)fia), especially of Ravenna (S. Maria in Cosmedin, chele in Affricisco—with figures of Justinian, Maxi- ;, and Theodora—and S. Apollinare Nuovo), and later nice (S. Marco), have a dignity and even beauty of wn, they are yet the living expression of the age, their formalised, but yet they live. It is true the voice of

▲

the antique art sounds feeble and strangely in this f world; the naked genii are now transformed to drape(long-winged angels—the martyrs and confessors who ad in long procession from the towered palace of the Ostro the Empress Theodora with her purple, gold-fringed robe, her bejewelled diadem, move against the rich backgrou if benumbed, as if dwelling in some solemn dream.

But they have not yet reached the sterility of the artist, the long meagre figures, the large and ill-shaped the empty stare, the corpse-like expression of the Byzantine school.

The forms had become purely traditional, and in the 13th century the Byzantine style, with its traditional I was still supreme in Tuscany.

The art of the people was dead, and yet the life c people was very real and very living. Think of the ir life, of the passionate loves and hatreds and party fet those nascent communes of Italy, the early struggles of cities as Milan, Pisa, Florence, the enthusiasm of the Franciscan religious revival, and then consider whether s race was likely to remain content with this outworn Byza formalism.

Italy of the Renaissance was awakening already, afte long ages of barbarism and spoliation, and was feelin way to the individual expression of her craving for new and passing over the tentative efforts of Giunto da

Giunto da Pisa, 1202–58.
The Monk Jacobus, about 1225.
Margheitone d'Arezzo, 1216–93.

(Campo Santo, Pisa, upper church of S. Francesco, *l* note "Destruction of Simon Magus"), of the Flore Mosaicist Jacobus (Mosaics in Florentine Baptistery, ; altar tribune, date 1225), and of Margheritone d'A (note especially signed picture in National Gallery) may date the first definite effort towards a more natur art in the work of the Florentine Giovanni Cenni, k

Cimabue, 1240–1302.
Examples.

generally as Cimabue. His two great pictures of Ma(form the commencement of a new epoch in art; one i Accademia at Florence, the other in S. Maria Novella (transept of Capella Rucellai), in that city.

THE AWAKENING OF LIFE.

as great importance in the development of his style are
frescoes in the upper church of S. Francesco, at Assisi,
senting the life of S. Francis and different sacred subjects,
showing already the transition to the more naturalistic
od of Giotto; while the Uffizi, Louvre, and National
ery contain pictures attributed to him, and the mosaics
he Pisan Duomo may be assigned to him with some
inty.

ie story of Cimabue's Madonna being borne in triumph
igh the streets of Florence with trumpeters, and beneath
wer of garlands, to its home in the church of S. Maria
ella is of real interest and value—as pointing to the
siasm of the Florentines for things of beauty, and the
gnition of a new revelation in a method whose naturalism
is case it needs our careful study to analyse.

hardly less interest is the story which makes Giotto to
been found by the elder painter on the Tuscan hill-side,
ing on a stone an outline of the sheep he was tending,
having been carried away by him to work in his Florentine
ga.

iotto Bondone lived 1276–1337, his birth thus corre- Giotto
ding with the death of Niccola Pisano, whose work in Bondone,
evival of sculpture we shall have to notice. 1276–1337.

the course of a long and industrious life he filled Italy
work of the greatest value. He was the founder of a
ol, and in the freshness and vitality of his art, in the
licity of his dramatic treatment, and the balance and
er of his composition it was long before his influence Examples.
ed to be felt. In studying Giotto we should have to
first, perhaps, his early work in the upper church of
rancis of Assisi. Then the chapel of S. Maria dell'
a at Padua, a building which no student of Giotto's work
fford to neglect, since it is entirely filled with frescoes by
master, most typical and original in treatment, repre-
ng the Life of the Virgin and the History of Christ,
allegorical figures of Virtues and Vices. Santa Croce,

at Florence (Peruzzi, Bardi, and Baroncelli Chapels), cont
his frescoes of the story of S. Francis, of S. John Evange
etc. Then, again, in S. Francesco, of Assisi, are the Pas
and the allegories of S. Francis, containing figures of Pov
(cf. Dante's "Paradiso," Book XI., "Francesco e Povertá
" questi amanti Prendi "), Chastity, and Obedience, onc
his most important works. At Rome is the mosaic, from
design, of the Navicella (Ship of the Church), and at Na
were the frescoes in the convent of Santa Chiara, which I
now perished. Those of the "Incoronata" at Naples I
been attributed to him, but without sufficient evidence.
Florence, too, are his portraits in the chapel of the Pa
of the Podesta (Dante, Brunetto Latini), and the beaut
Campanile of her Duomo, that lasting monument of his ger
In this brief catalogue of Giotto's more important wo
which does not include those which have perished (S. (
vanni Laterano in Rome—portrait of Boniface VIII. surviv
—S. Antonio of Padua), or are still whitewashed (St
Croce, Florence), perhaps the most important, the most typ
for the student, are those frescoes,* just noticed, of the lo
church of Assisi, and of the Arena Chapel. In the for
Giotto appears under the influence of the great Francis
movement, and shows its conceptions most typically in
marriage of S. Francis with Poverty,—inspired, perhaps
the lines from Dante's "Paradiso" quoted above,—wl
Christ joins the hands of these two lovers while angels we
their union, where the rich with their money bags turn be
where elsewhere Chastity sits in her fortress, adored by ang
In the church of S. Maria dell' Arena he appears rather
a great innovator, and beneath the blue arched vault, stud
with golden stars, takes us through the whole cycle of
history of the Virgin, and of Christ, creates new ty
everywhere which became later almost traditional,† and
each and every subject with the intensity of his own im:
native conviction, with the new breath of real life which
brought into art.

* V., Appendix I. † V., Appendix IV.

[By Giotto
'ondone] S. CLARA AT THE DEATH [S. Francesco
OF S. FRANCIS. of Assisi.
(Fotog. Anderson.)

By Giotto Bondone]   A WINDOW OF GIOTTO'S CAMPANILE.   [DUOMO OF FLORENCE.

That Giotto gave to art, it has been well said, was, before things, vitality. "His Madonnas are no longer symbols of a certain phase of pious awe, but pictures of maternal love. . . . . Nor was the change less in his method than his motives. Before his day painting had been without composition, without charm of colour, without suggestion of movement or the play of living energy. He first knew how to distribute figures in the given space with perfect balance, and how to mass them together in animated groups agreeable to the eye. He caught varied and transient shades of emotion, and expressed them by the posture of the body and the play of feature."

The two points mentioned here, the vitality of his art, and masterfulness of his composition, I would urge upon the attention of the student of his work; the beauty of his drapery, with its severe and simple folds, the dramatic vividness of his pictured stories must be noticed here.

In the aim to express ideal beauty he is perhaps surpassed by the Sienese; he has already the Florentine interest in personal portraiture, the Florentine love of design.

These are qualities which lift him above his historical position, which is itself unique, into one of the great masters of all time; they are expressed in these frescoes of the Church of Santa Croce, in which I can only briefly allude here to the noble beauty of Santa Chiara, to the dying S. Francis surrounded by his disciples, to the graceful figure of the violin player in the dance of Herodias, and that group of two young girls behind the dancer who clasp one another with the most natural and most charming naïveté of movement.

In his work around the Campanile of Santa Maria del Fiore he transmitted his influence to the sculpture of his epoch; and under his influence was completed the façade of the cathedral which has perished.

Mr. Leader Scott remarks of this in his interesting work on the Italian Renaissance :—" Giotto's front, which consisted of several tiers of pillared arches filled with statues, may still be seen in a fresco by Poccetti in the first cloister of

" S. Marco. Its statues were by Andrea Pisano and of
" artists of the day. . . . The four evangelists w
" seated in grand niches round the principal door, and abo
" under a beautiful Gothic canopy, was placed a marble gr
" of the Virgin and Child, between S. Zanobio and S.
" parata, the two Florentine patron saints ; two angels h
" the curtains." Above the entrance to the left was a gr
of the Nativity, and on the right a Pietà, while other fig
were of saints, churchmen, politicians, and literati, " an
" rangement significant of the reverence in which power
" learning were held by the Florentines of the 14th centu
This beautiful façade was destroyed by the Florentines
1586 to make room for " the hideous Renaissance front
Buonaccorsi, which was, fortunately, never erected.

In the bas-reliefs after his designs at the base of his C
panile, treating of the creation of man and the discover
the arts, &c., he was assisted by Andrea di Pontedera,
worked upon his designs.

To treat of these adequately we are obliged here to ret
our steps so as to grasp the first beginnings of P
sculpture.

This may be said to commence with *Niccola Pisano*,
appears in Pisa in the early XIIIth century.

Niccola is, indeed, as distinctively the maker of a new ep
in Italian sculpture as Cimabue or yet more Giotto in
painting. Almost all we know about him, it has b
remarked, is derived from a couple of inscriptions, a
contracts, and his life by Giorgio Vasari. Yet we h
remaining to us his work, the most precious commentary
the influences which he came under, on the ideas which
endeavoured to express.

To take this in order, we must commence with the " D
sition from the Cross " (about 1233-37) over one of
doors of S. Martino at Lucca.

He had studied that sarcophagus which yet remains to
in the Campo Santo of Pisa, which had once indeed conta
the dust of Beatrice, mother of the Countess Matilda, a

THE AWAKENING OF LIFE. 7

...assic times, which bore upon it, carved in relief, the story ...ippolytus and Phaedra. " Studying the heroic nudities ...d noble attitudes of this bas-relief, Niccola rediscovered ...e right way of art, not by merely copying his model, but ... divining the secret of the grand style."
...he results of this research appears already in the dignity ... breadth of treatment of the sculpture, carved in high ...f, at S. Martino, the cathedral church of Lucca. It is yet ...e marked in his celebrated pulpit in the Baptistery of Pisa. ...had derived further help from the study of a marble vase, ...ed with Bacchus and his train of Maenads, and in these ...eful forms had already touched the inspiration of Renais-...e art.
...ence we find that in his "Adoration of the Magi," carved ...n the Pisan pulpit, Madonna carries herself as haughtily ...Theseus' wife; while Mr. Symonds traces in the High ...est of the Circumcision the majesty of Dionysus, and finds ... naked vigour of Hippolytus in the Hercules or Fortitude ...n a bracket of the pulpit.
 These sculptures of Pisano are thus for us a symbol of ...t happened in the age of the Revival.
 The old world and the new shook hands; Christianity ... Hellenism kissed each other. And yet they still remained ...agonistic, fused externally by art, but severed in the ...sciousness that, during these strange years of dubious ...ulse, felt the might of both."
?rom Pisa Niccola is summoned to Siena, to carve a pulpit ... the Duomo, commenced in that century; the contract ...ich he signed with Fra Melano, the capo-maestro of the ...rks of the Duomo, is still extant.
...Ie was to receive 65 Pisan pounds for the marble required, ... pupils six Pisan " solidos " a day, besides bed and lodging. ...ese pupils were Arnolfo and Lapo; his son Giovanni was ...eceive half as much as his father. The pulpit of octagonal ...n rested upon nine columns, supported either by lions and ...esses or figures carved in marble; the bas-reliefs repre-...ted the Nativity, Adoration of the Magi, and other

Scriptural subjects, concluding with the Crucifixion and Judgment. Here, as at Pisa, he combines feeling fo antique beauty with an effort towards naturalism of treat yet with less success than in the former monument ; the efforts clash and weaken the result, though in the Judgment the nude figures are remarkable for their vigo action and movement.

The shrine of S. Dominic at Bologna, and the bea fountain at Perugia belong more properly to his pupi Fra Guglielmo in the former case, to Giovanni Pisano ii latter.

But to Niccola himself belongs all the initiative o: movement ; his appearance in Pisa in this century, and definite classicism of his style, has been traced by C and Cavalcaselle not merely to the study of the few ant to be found in Pisa, but to the possible fact of his hi migrated from Apulia, where in the 13th century a s of sculpture already existed.

These authors trace the resemblance of his work to of Nicholas de Bartolommeus of Foggia, whose bu: Sigalgaita Rufolo at Ravello, near the republic of A₁ at that time on good terms with Pisa, is classical in fe and similar to the work of Niccola in technique. F₁ was, in the 13th century, the ordinary residence of Fre the Second, his palace there being erected in 1233, a would be interesting to ascertain if this monarch, s₁ beyond his time in his culture and his aims, had contri indirectly even to the great revival of plastic art.

I merely state this theory as one of great interest ; b any case the relation of Niccola to that revival is o utmost importance.

" Conventional as Niccola's manner was," say the au just quoted, " it could not but create emulation and ri " in the study of mere form ; and the examples of Pi " this sense were of advantage to all the schools of ⁂ " But while Niccola infused a new spirit into the ₁

PULPIT OF THE DUOMO OF SIENA.

BY NICCOLA PISANO.

(*See p.* 7.)

his countrymen he could lay no claim to the creation of
ristian types.

Iis art, had it remained unsupported by the new current
ligious and political thought so sensible in the 13th
·y, would perhaps have perished without leaving a trace
l it. Mere classical imitation could not suffice for the
of the time; and thus it was that while Niccola
d on one side an emulation that was to produce the
t fruits, he was himself convinced that, without a return
study of nature, no progress was possible. In his
)t to graft on the conventional imitation of the antique
ly of nature he failed; nor would his son and pupils
succeeded, even in the measure which is visible in their
, but for the examples which were created for them
ther and greater school—the Florentine."

s new influence is more visible in the work of Niccola's
iovanni than in that of his elder pupil, Fra Guglielmo.

this latter artist must be assigned the bas-reliefs of the Fra Guglielmo,
)f S. Domenico at Bologna, where the mortal remains worked from 1257-1313.
t saint were now contained.

se bas-reliefs depicted various incidents in the life of Examples.
minic and his disciples. "Fra Guglielmo, in the exe-
on of these subjects, preserved, but enfeebled, the style
Niccola—imparted to the figures but little character,
:ession, or design—overcharged the draperies and
rded the groups."

ble, as a monk of that order, to claim any pay for his
·s, he is said to have found a consolation in helping
f to a bone of the deceased saint: the theft was not
ered till he confessed it at his death, and overjoyed
ithren of S. Catherine at Pisa with the news that they
sed one rib of S. Dominic. At Pistoja Fra Guglielmo
robably employed on the pulpit of S. Giovanni Fuor-
, and later was at work on the loggia of the Duomo
rieto; he died, as I have related, in the convent of
herine at Pisa.

Giovanni Pisano, worked from 1264-1320. Examples.

A better exponent of the new influences at work, as fi their expression in Italian sculpture, is Giovanni Pisa whom I have already alluded. In the fountain of Pe he exhibits qualities of a different character to those c father Niccola, and of a character even superior; architect he worked on the Campo Santo at Pisa, an decorative ornament of S. Maria della Spina in that while for several years he held the position of capo-m of the works at the Duomo of Siena. His masterpiec been considered the pulpit of S. Andrea at Pistoja.
" superiority of that complex and consummate work of p
" art," says Mr. Symonds, " over the pulpit of the
" Baptistery in all the most important qualities of styl
" composition, can scarcely be called in question. Its
" serious fault is an exaggeration of the height of the
" in proportion to the size of the hexagon they su
" Like the pulpits of the Baptistery of the Duomo of
" and of the Duomo of Siena, it combines bas-relie
" detached statues, carved capitals, and sculptured li
" a maze of marvellous invention; but it has no rival
" architectural effect of harmony, and the masterly feeli
" balanced masses it displays."

The subjects which Giovanni had chosen for his bas were "The Nativity," the "Adoration of the Magi "Massacre of the Innocents," the "Crucifixion," a "Last Judgment," but he approached his subject in a r different to that of Niccola.

His young and graceful Madonna has nothing, as Sy points out again, of the Roman mother of Niccola' ception, his vivid Massacre, with its men and even defying and cursing the enthroned tyrant, shows an in of conception, a stir of passionate life that takes us awa the calmer types of the classic past.

" He effected a fusion between the grand style revi Niccola and the romantic fervour of the modern imagi It was in this way that the tradition handed down proved inestimably serviceable to the painters."

his conception as an architect is due that treasure house
rteenth century Italian art, the Campo Santo of Pisa
hundred feet in length he planned it and one hundred
venty in width, bounded by a high wall, which enclosed
red cloister or arcade, while the open burial ground in
ntre was filled with earth carried from the Holy Land.
n this arcade there came to be painted later a whole series
scoes, typical in their qualities and invaluable in their
rom the less interesting work of the Florentine Buffal-
(Passion of Christ, Resurrection, &c., east wall) to the
ls of Job," by Francesco Volterra, to the "Lives of
Ephesus and Potitus" of Spinello, to the tremendous
mph of Death" and "Hell" and "Heaven," attributed
Lorenzetti (south wall), even to the dainty grace of
zo's later frescoes; the whole forms a priceless col-
h of early Italian art, to which we shall have again and
to refer the reader's interest. A later work by Giovanni
he pulpit of the Cathedral of Pisa, now unhappily
h up. "An interesting fragment, one of the supporting
mns of the octagon which formed the body of the struc-
, still exists in the Museum of the Campo Santo. It
an allegorical statue of Pisa. The Ghibelline city is
sonified as a crowned woman, suckling children at her
ist, and standing on a pedestal supported by the eagle
the Empire. She wears a girdle of rope seven times
tted, to betoken the rule of Pisa over seven subject
ds. At the four corners of her throne stand the four
an virtues, Prudence, Temperance, Justice, and Forti-
, distinguished less by beauty of shape than by deter-
ed energy of symbolism. Temperance is a naked
an, with hair twisted in the knots and curls of a Greek
rodite. Justice is old and wrinkled, clothed with
sive drapery, and holding in her hands the scales."
gh all this work of the Pisan artist, as in his beautiful
of Pope Benedict XI. at S. Domenico in Perugia, where
g angels draw back the curtains that shield the dead
long slumber, there breathes a spirit alien to the purely

classic sentiment of Niccola, the spirit of the great Chri[stian] revival, initiated by the teaching of S. Francis, and whic[h] Giotto's work was to find in these years so perfect a pict[orial] expression.

Sculpture, the minister of form, steps aside for the mo[ment] from her high place, and seeks from her sister art an initi[ation] in symbolism or in facial expression.

"Italian sculpture abandoned the presentation of the n[ude] human body as useless. The emotions written on the [face] became of more importance than the modelling of the li[mbs] and recourse was had to allegorical symbols or embler[matic] attitudes for the interpretation of the artist's thought."

Like Orcagna later, Giovanni was employed on the relief on the front of the Orvieto Cathedral, commenc[ed] 1290, but it is difficult here to differentiate his work [from] that of Andrea Pisano and others of Niccola's followers. [He] died in 1320, and was buried in the Campo Santo of Pi[sa by] the side of his father.

Already Italian sculpture had come decidedly unde[r] Florentine influence, and in the work of Andrea Pisano [on] Giotto's designs we shall find their influence definitely [esta]blished. But before pursuing this development, I wish [once] again to turn back, and briefly gather up the remaining t[hread] of artistic progress, in glancing at the work of the S[ienese] artists.

The Sienese School. I may have at the same time to allude to the sister st[ates of] Lucca and Arezzo; but it is Siena, the rival at this [time] of Florence (1260 and onwards), that claims most [of our] interest.

A very early altar piece (Virgin and Child) by a [certain] Guido de Senis (of Siena) is in S. Domenico in that city [with] the date 1221, a date which encouraged the Sienese to [claim] a priority of time over Florence in the revival of pa[inting]. Guido has also some doubtful panels in the Siena galler[y, but] the first master of this school who developed an ind[ividual]

THE AWAKENING OF LIFE. 13

nd gave an impulse to creative art is Duccio di Buonin- Duccio di
who lived as a contemporary with Dietisalvi in the end Buoninsegna, about 1270–
13th century. 1339.
great altar-piece of the Majesty of the Virgin was
ed from 1308–10, and, like the Madonna of Cimabue,
irried in procession through the town by the clergy,
ie Archbishop at their head, with the magistrates of the
ne, the chief men of the Monte de' Nove, and the
rs of the city with their wives and children, to rest at
in its place of honour within the cathedral.
iccio's altar-piece presented on one face to the spectator
;in seated with the Infant Christ upon her lap, and
ig the homage of the patron saint of Siena. On the
ie depicted the principal scenes of the Gospel story,
e Passion of Our Lord, in 28 compartments. What
ieculiar value to this elaborate work of Sienese art is,
it Duccio managed to combine the tradition of an early
? style of painting with all the charm of brilliant
ng, and with dramatic force of presentation only rivalled
time by Giotto.
dependently of Giotto, he performed at a stroke what
ie and his pupil had achieved for the Florentines, and
thed to the succeeding painters of Siena a tradition of
ond which they rarely passed."
:io is well represented in the National Gallery (cf. his
sfiguration " and his charming " Annunciation "), and
ismo Monkhouse, in his recent work on that collection,
ioticing this painter's pure transparent colouring and
il type with oval face, and rather long limbs, remarks :
illowed his own temperament, and by so doing deter-
the characteristics of the Sienese school, which stands
swhat the same relation to that of Florence as a woman
in.
is signed altar piece of the Florence Academy he shows
me softness and transparency of colouring, the same
ual qualities ; while of less interest is the work of the

Sienese Segna di Buonaventura, shown in his quaint a piece (Virgin and Child with donors), at Castiglione Fiorent and his "Crucifixion" of the National Gallery.

The Lorenzetti (Ambrogio and Pietro), worked— Ambrogio, 1324-45; Pietro, 1305-48. Examples.

This tradition of art, which was developed in the worl the Lorenzetti (Ambrogio and Pietro) and of Simone Mem places the Sienese school as distinct from, and almost a ri of, the Florentine.

The Lorenzetti painted, about the year 1340, that "Lif(the Hermits in the Thebaid" which is in the Campo Sa of Pisa, beside the famous "Triumph of Death" of Orcag to Pietro Lorenzetti is also due the Madonna and Saints S. Ansano (Siena), a painting dated 1340 in the Uffizi, ar powerful series of frescoes in the lower church of S. Franc at Assisi, representing the history of our Lord; and Ambrogio the great symbolical frescoes in the Pale Pubblico at Siena, setting forth the consequences of g and evil government, and completed the 18th February 13:

Of great interest are these frescoes of the "Sala dei N e della Pace," in which the mediæval commune finds its 1 pictorial expression. Enthroned and crowned sits the fig of Government, a robed and white-bearded man, while be him wait Peace, Fortitude, and Prudence, and on his hand Magnanimity, Temperance, and Justice, while bene is the throng of burghers, and mailed knights sit on horseba at guard with their spears upraised. Not easily forgotter the exquisite figure of "Peace," of an almost Greek bea of type and form, with her feet resting on the helm shield, and taken, men have said, from an ancient sta found near Siena. Elsewhere we see the consequences misgovernment and faction, which Siena knew too w and the whole is a representation of the mediæval concep of life, marvellous in its mastery and breadth of treatm only to be compared with the Pisan "Triumph of Dea which might well be from the same firm hand.

Simone Memmi, 1283-1344.

In the same Palazzo Pubblico, Simone Martini, be known as Simone Memmi, had painted in fresco a g

THE AWAKENING OF LIFE. 15

:ture of the Virgin Enthroned and surrounded by Saints, *Examples.*
d in the chapel of S. Martin in S. Francesco of Assisi had
)duced one of his greatest works—the legend of that Saint
10 pictures. He painted with softer feeling of beauty *Ugolino da*
in even Duccio, and we may, perhaps, trace the transition *Siena, early*
m one to the other method in the work of Ugolino da *14th century.*
:na (portions of altar-piece now in National Gallery).
Simone painted also altar-pieces for the Dominicans of *Simone*
Catherine at Pisa and for the altar of S. Domenico at *Memmi—*
vieto ; but it is by the frescos I have mentioned that *continued.*
none will be best remembered.

'n his paintings Mr. Symonds has traced the hand of an
[uisite and patient craftsman, elaborately careful to finish
 work with the utmost refinement, sensitive to feminine
.uty, full of delicate inventiveness, and gifted with a rare
ling for grace.

3ut these very qualities tend in themselves toward over-
;ness, and even affectation. As in all the Sienese school,
re is lacking the firm drawing, the touch of vigorous
illectualism which Florence sought after and maintained.
[olles Senae "—it has been well said of Simone—" the
elicate and feminely variable, fond of all things brilliant,
nd unstable through defect of sternness, was the fit mother
f this ingenious and delightful master."

ndeed, the sentiment of beauty lives through the work
this artist, who, perhaps, had portrayed the Laura of
rarch (as it does throughout the Sienese school), and
rloads it sometimes with a certain affectation. In his
it work in the Palazzo Pubblico, "the Virgin, wearing
 diadem over her veil of blue, sits on a throne and grace-
illy calls attention, by a gesture of her right hand, to the
nfant Saviour standing upon her knee and supported by
er left arm. Her ample dress, minutely engraved with
olden arabesques, luxuriously and somewhat studiously
othes a form more feminine and elegant than majestic.
. certain affectation clings to her and is perceptible in the

THE AWAKENING OF LIFE.

"movement of the frame as well as in the action
"beautiful hand." In our account of his work the fres
painted in 1328 in the Sala del Consiglio of Siena, and
taining the portrait of the victor of Montemassi and S
Forte, Guidoriccio Fogliani de Ricci, must not be forgotte

Margaritone, born about 1236. Meanwhile at Arezzo an early initiative had been give painting by the work of Margaritone, mentioned already,

Montano d'Arezzo, worked from 1305. painted in the early manner of the *trecentisti*, and by Mon d'Arezzo, who attained some celebrity and painted cer chapels in the Castel del' Uovo for King Robert of Na

Lippo Memmi, worked from 1317-56. Examples. Returning to the Sienese, we find Lippo Memmi engage fresco work at San Gimignano in style analogous to Sin (Palazzo del Podestá at San Gimignano, and perhaps S. A tino at Siena), and at Orvieto, where a Virgin with supplic (S. Corporale) has the legend "Lippi, native of the plea Siena, painted us"; and in Siena herself Taddeo di Ba

Taddeo di Bartolo, 1362-1422. Examples. continuing the tradition of Duccio's painting, and paintin 1406 the chapel of the Palazzo Pubblico, as well as a adjoining (1414).

His most interesting work, however, is in the churc S. Francesco of Pisa, painted for Donna Datuccia of the S family, in which there is a fresco representing the Apo visiting the Virgin, who is seated in an open loggia, v her visitors descend to her from heaven, and one who already alighted kneels before her in adoration.

Spinello Aretino, about 1333-1410. In Spinello Aretino this sense of divine motion bec quickened in his magnificent Gabriel, "rushing down "heaven to salute Madonna, with all the whirr of "angelic pinions and the glory of Paradise around him."

Trained under Spinello Aretino were his son, Parri Spi (1387-1452), who has left relics of his art at Arezzo, his scholar, Niccolo di Pietro Gerini (frescoes of cha house of S. Bonaventura, Pisa, and at Prato); but neith these could compare in technique or imagination with teacher, Spinello himself.

Examples. In the chapel of S. Agostino at Arezzo he had painted Annunciation, and in her cathedral a Christ crucified, w

s been much repainted; on the south wall of the Campo
nto of Pisa he had painted in fresco, with great beauty
sentiment, the legend of S. Ephesus. He loved battles
d the clash of steel-clad knights, and in the Sala di Balia
Siena had depicted the struggle of the communes against
ederic Barbarossa; "few faces," it has been said of his
scoes in Pisa, "in the painting of any period are more
fascinating than the profiles under steel-blue battle-caps of
that godlike pair—the knightly saint and the Archangel
Michael—breaking by the irresistible force of their onset
and their calm youthful beauty through the mailed ranks
of the Sardinian pagans." Having thus far followed the
ools of painting which took their rise in Arezzo and Siena,
have to return again to follow out the influence of Giotto
it developed itself in Florence.

To a late epoch belongs the work of Domenico di Bartolo Matteo di
nels dated 1433 and 1438 in Academy of Siena), of his Giovanni di
Bartolo,
temporary, Lorenzo di Pietro (remains of frescoes in called Matteo
lazzo Pubblico, Siena, and Virgin and Child, dated 1457, in di Siena, about
1435-95.
fizi), and of Matteo da Siena, born about 1435, who has at
na his altar-piece, the "Madonna della Neve," in which
gels bear vases filled with snow, while others roll up
wballs (dated 1477), his picture of S. Barbara executed in
same year (S. Domenico), and his pictures of the Murder
he Innocents (S. Agostino and Concezione), a subject alien
is feeling for dreamy, delicate beauty. Far better is he in
National Gallery picture, the Virgin rising to Heaven,
le S. Thomas receives her girdle, with its lovely naïve
els in rich garments of silk and brocade. Matteo was the
Sienese painter who developed the specific traditions of
cio, and with him our notice of that school may find an
ropriate ending.

n the Sienese, as, indeed, later in all the Umbrian school,
trace something of the character of her citizens, now
ged into the fury of murderous civil dissensions, now
ed to passionate piety by the eloquence of a S. Bernardino;

B

an art more passionate, more emotional, less scientific, and intellectual than the Florentine shows itself from the fir these cities of Umbria—an art, therefore, less durable sane, less capable of continuance, but not the less fu interest and beauty. We shall see later how this continuing its tradition through the work of the Peri school, was to find at length its completeness in the marve personality of Rafaelle, brought by his training alike 1 both influences, and summing, as it were, in himself alik intellect and the emotion, the completest, and, in that ʁ the highest expression of the art of the Renaissance.

Yet, returning now to Florence towards the middle o 14th century, we find that Giotto's death had left a gap ᴠ

Taddeo Gaddi, 1300-66.
could not easily be filled. Taddeo Gaddi had been bou him as his godson by family ties, and as an artist had most directly under his influence. Yet Taddeo, when ask name the greatest painter of Italy, had said, " Since Gi death art has fallen very low."

Examples.
Taddeo indeed was himself but a reflex of his gɪ teacher ; his work in the Baroncelli Chapel of Santa (at Florence (frescoes representing the Life of the V given to Taddeo by Vasari), though fine in compositioɪ been characterised as conventional in expression, move and execution.

" Taddeo's execution was, in fact, rapid, decorative conventional; yet to a distant observer his style was eff and sometimes imposing.

" Lower than Giotto in the scale of art, he was essen inferior to him in rendering character and expression—lɑ at once his softness and gravity, his elegance and ɛ simplicity."

Santa Croce, which during the 14th century was with his frescoes as well as those of Giotto, and in cloisters he was buried, now contains in her refect " cenacolo " attributed to him, besides a Crucifixion. Pisa some of his frescoes remain in the church of S. Fran

THE AWAKENING OF LIFE.

[A]nd every visitor to Florence who is interested in art will [re]member the great frescoes in the Capellone dei Spagnuoli [of] S. Maria Novella, attributed to this artist working in [con]junction with Simone Memmi of Siena.

Vasari is responsible for this view of their authorship, and [giv]es a detailed description of the fresco in his Life of [Gi]otto; but this view has been disputed by modern critics, [and] Messrs. Crowe and Cavalcaselle seem more disposed to [att]ribute these frescoes to Andrea de Florentiâ.

The subject, the Church Triumphant and Militant, has been [bea]utifully described by Mr. Ruskin; the Dominicans who, as [bla]ck and white dogs, hunt down the heretics, the numerous [por]traits introduced, Boccaccio, Laura, Cimabue, and others, [giv]e the fresco on the right wall an especial interest.

[I]f we see Giotto's influence continued in painting in the [wor]k of Taddeo, we find it again in the sculpture of Andrea [P]ontedera, who worked under Giotto's directions, and from [his] designs on the bas-reliefs around the Campanile of Santa [Ma]ria del Fiore. In the form of a series of hexagons these [bas-]reliefs represent to us the creation of the human race, [and] its first triumphs over the conditions in which it was [pla]ced.

Andrea di Pontedera, worked from 1305 to about 1360.

Beautiful and full of dignity is the naked form of Eve as [she] is drawn by the Creator from the sleeping man, and later [we] find Jubal occupied on music, Noah's discovery of wine, [ma]n taming the horse or destroying wild beasts, and woman [alr]eady busy at the loom.

Not less beautiful, nor less impregnated with the sentiment [of G]iotto, so exquisite in its naïf simplicity, are the reliefs on [the] southern door of the Florentine Baptistery, representing [the] history of S. John and the eight cardinal virtues; it is [in t]hese latter figures that the student who has come to [app]reciate the great qualities of the Florentine master, will [find] them in all their charm, a charm which he may perhaps [seek] vainly in the maturer work of a later era.

THE AWAKENING OF LIFE.

"The finest nude of the 14th century," it has remarked, "is that of the Saviour in the baptism of bronze gates; the most pleasing composition in the series is the Salutation. The former is a figure which perfection of modelling, breadth of drapery, and beaut shape, rivals the Redeemer of the Baptistery of Rav(The art of Giotto, pre-eminent in painting and in a tecture, thus appears equally so in sculpture, which, th carried out by the hands of another, is vivified by spirit. It is the greatest monument of the rise o: 14th century, and gives final polish to the art of Pisa."

Andrea had worked for several years on the sculptur
Nino Pisano, worked from about 1350. Orvieto in company with his son Nino; and after his fat death Nino Pisano appears to have returned to Pisa, v the half figure by his hand of the Virgin giving the brea the Infant Christ on the front of S. Maria della Spina is of naturalistic effort, though preserving the Giottesque and fineness of draperies.

The standing figures of Virgin and Child between S. . and S. John, beside the high altar of this church, are from Nino's chisel, and are to be noted for their grace for the finish of the workmanship; he worked also on
The Giottesques: Puccio Capanna, worked from 1350. tombs of the Archbishop of Pisa, Simone Salterelli, a Giovanni dell' Agnello de' Conti. Meanwhile the tra of Giotto's painting was continued by such craftsme Puccio Capanna (Ufizzi Gallery, Christ Crucified, and L S. Louis and other saints at S. Francesco al Prato of Pis
Francesco da Volterra, worked from 1346. Giottino, about 1325-95. mentioned by Vasari, Ottaviano and Pace of Faenza, Pe Rimini, and that Francesco da Volterra to whom are ass the frescoes of the trials of Job, on the south wall o Campo Santo of Pisa. In Florence and at Assisi the known as Giottino—possibly Tommaso di Stefano—ha work which follows out the spirit of his teacher Giotto. vaults of the Strozzi family, beneath the Capellon Spagnuoli in S. Maria Novella, the chapel of S. Silves S. Croce, and, at Assisi, the Capella del Sagramento i

·ch of S. Francesco, contain the best remaining examples
is work.
t the same time with Giottino may be noticed Bernardo di Bernardo
do, who has been confused with Nardo Cione, Orcagna's di Daddo, died 1350.
r brother, and who has a triptych in the Florence
demy (signed Bernardus de Florentia) and two panels at
ιa. I shall notice later the theory which would make him
author of the Pisan (Campo Santo) frescoes. Francesco
ni has two altar-pieces (one dated 1346), and Jacopo da
entino (born about 1310) followed Taddeo Gaddi from the
entino to Florence, worked in a Giottesque manner on the
s and ceiling of Or San Michele, and has an interesting
:-piece, now in the National Gallery of London. He has
ner the honour of having founded the Guild of Painters in
ence (in 1349), and having had Spinello Aretino as his
ılar ; while the work of the Bicci family in three genera-
s, Lorenzo di Bicci, Bicci di Lorenzo, and Nero di Bicci
1 1486), shows the gradual decadence of the Giottesque
ition.
hus we find that, even after Giotto's death, among a
le school of artists his influence remained paramount. As
Symonds has remarked :—" The Gaddi of Florence,
iottino, Puccio Capanna, the Lorenzetti of Siena, Spinello
Arezzo, Andrea Orcagna, Domenico Veneziano, and the
sser artists of the Pisan Campo Santo, were either formed
influenced by him. To give account of the frescoes of
ese painters would be to describe how the religious,
ıcial, and philosophical conceptions of the 14th century
und complete expression in form and colour. By means
allegory and pictured scene they drew the portrait of the
iddle Age in Italy, performing jointly and in combination
ith the followers of Niccola Pisano what Dante had done
ngly by his poetry."
efore, however, I leave these artists of the school of Andrea
:to, I must pause awhile over the work of one of the Orcagna, about 1308-68
test and most original among them, that of Andrea or 69,
ıgnuolo di Cione, more generally known as Orcagna.

Andrea Orcagna stands alone among the Giottesques by originality and power of his genius. At once a pai sculptor, and architect, he stands out as one of the g personalities of the Italian revival, and though affected Giotto, was never dominated by him as were the lesser 1 He was indeed far above such artists as the Gaddi, and ra returned to the high vantage ground, the simplicity strength, which Giotto Bondone had exhibited.

Orcagna was a pupil of Andrea Pisano, and had studied goldsmith's art under his father Cione. As a painter remains famous for his frescoes, especially those within Strozzi Chapel in S. Maria Novella at Florence, where he adorned the choir with frescoes, which have been since repl by those of Ghirlandajo; as a sculptor and worker in meta is most celebrated for the tabernacle of Or San Michele, for by him to enshrine the Madonna of Ugolino da Siena.

To be noticed by the student of the English Nati Gallery is his great altar-piece, with nine attendant pictu painted originally for S. Pietro Maggiori in Florence, inf certainly to the frescoes I have just mentioned, but yet freshness and beauty in the forms of the playing and sin angels.

He was also engaged for some time as Capo-maestro of works on the Duomo of Orvieto, and his great fresc the "Triumph of Death," in the Campo Santo of Pisa, work of the most terrible power of dramatic express though in this last case I must add that it has been questi by some critics whether to himself or to the Lorenzetti sh be attributed the authorship of this great imaginative wor

His greatness as a fresco-painter may in any case secu rest upon his work in the Strozzi Chapel of S. Maria Nov where in his Paradise the blessed stand ranked—"pr after profile laid together like lilies in a garden border beneath where Madonna rests in sweet repose, bo reverently towards the throne of the triumphant Christ.

Here the purity of his drawing, the ideal beauty of types become apparent. In his Inferno he had followed

?ful student the outlines given to his age in Dante's
'nmedia, and had yet approached the subject with
;inality and vigour of conception.
Iis power is not less apparent in his work on the taber-
⁰le of Or San Michele, though expressed in a totally different
terial; as early as 1355 he had been appointed Capo-
3stro to this oratory, "one of the great monuments of
nixed architecture, sculpture, and mosaics of the time, the
abernacle of which was executed from his designs."
n this wonderful shrine, which suffers perhaps from want
space and light in its present position, Orcagna shows the
ver and breadth of his craftsmanship in sculpture, as else-
ere in painting. The whole is indeed a "monumental
el," complete in its unity of conception, even, as it has
u remarked, to the very iron rail which enclosed the shrine.
the subjects of the Annunciation, the Nativity, the Marriage
the Virgin, and the Adoration of the Three Kings, framed
octagonal mouldings at the base of the tabernacle, has
n traced the domination of a spirit distinct both from the
'-Romanism of Niccola and the Gothicism of Giovanni
'ano.
'That spirit is Florentine in a general sense, and speci-
lly Giottesque. Charity, again, with a flaming heart in
hand, crowned with a flaming brazier, and suckling a
ld, is Giottesque, not only in allegorical conception, but
o in choice of type and treatment of drapery."
[must pause before those powerful frescoes in the Campo
ita of Pisa, attributed by Vasari to Orcagna, and which are,
my case, among the most remarkable productions of his
ich. Without detailing the dispute as to the authorship,
may state briefly that Vasari stated Orcagna to be their
uter, but his brother, Nardo, to have finished the "Inferno";
t Crowe and Cavalcaselle, finding a style more Sienese than
)rentine (especially in "S. Macarius and the Hermits"),
ve the authorship to the Lorenzetti, while Signor Milanesi
s suggested Bernardo Daddi (died 1350). In any case, they

are intended to depict " the advantages of contemplative o
" active life, suggesting that, whereas in the pursuit
" pleasure, and in the enjoyment of wealth, death invaria
" takes the common mortal by surprise ; on the contrary,
" lowly hermit expects it without fear, and welcomes
" approach."

Hence, we see on the right of the fresco a party of knig
and ladies going hawking, who pause, however, before th
open graves filled with half-decaying corpses ; behind are
hermits living their life of abnegation among the birds ɑ
beasts in the rocks. On the other side of the fresco aɪ
group of youths and maidens such as Boccacio has depicted
his *Decameron*, yet stricken here by the cruel scythe of Deɑ
while in the centre the maimed and wretched implore releasᴇ
but in vain—from their life. " Thus, to the awakening ɑ
" of the Italians," says Mr. Symonds, " on the threshold
" the modern era, with the sonnets of Petrarch and the stoɪ
" of Boccaccio sounding in their memories, this terrible maɛ
" presented the three saddest phantoms of the Middle Ageɪ
" the spectre of death omnipotent, the solitude of the deɛ
" as the only refuge from a sinful and doomed world,
" dread of divine justice inexorable and inevitable."

" In those piles of the promiscuous and abandoned dᴇ
those fiends and angels poised in mid-air struggling for so
those blind and mutilated beggars vainly besieging De
with prayers and imprecations for deliverance, while
descends in her robe of woven wire to mow down with
scythe the knights and ladies in their garden of deligɪ
again, in those horses snuffing at the open graves, th
countesses and princes face to face with skeletons, th
serpents coiling round the flesh of what was once fair yo
and maid . . . . in all this terrible amalgamationɪ
sinster and tragic ideas, vividly presented, full of coɑ
dramatic power, and intensified by faith in their mateɪ
reality, the Lorenzetti brethren, if theirs be indeed the haɪ
that painted here, summed up the nightmares of the Mid

THE AWAKENING OF LIFE.

…es and bequeathed an ever-memorable picture of its desolate …occupations to the rising world.

"They have called to their aid poetry, and history, and …end.

"Boccaccio supplies them with the garden scene of youths … damsels dancing among roses while the plague is at …ir gates and death is in the air above. From Petrarch …y have borrowed the form and mystic robe of Death …self. Uguccione della Faggiuola has sat for the portrait … the captain who must quail before the terrors of the …nb, and Castruccio Castracane is the strong man cut off … the blossom of his age. The prisons of the Visconti have …gorged their victims, cast adrift with maiming that makes … unendurable, but does not hasten death. The lazar …uses and the charnels have been ransacked for forms of …sly decay. Thus the whole work is not merely 'an …roglyphical and shadowed lesson' of ascetic philosophy; … is also a realization of mediæval life in its cruellest …ensity and most uncompromising truth. . . . Studying …se frescoes, we cannot but reflect what nerves, what brains, …at hearts encased in triple brass the men who thought and … thus must have possessed. They make us comprehend …t merely the stern and savage temper of the Middle Ages, …t the intense and fiery ebullition of the Renaissance, into …ich, as by a sudden liberation, so much imprisoned, pent-up …ce was driven."

And, indeed, it is to this Renaissance itself, in all the …thusiasm of its first effort, that we are now approaching; …I have quoted at some length from the above description … this great mediæval fresco, it has been not only for the …uty of its language, but also for the value of the work …lf as typifying a class of ideas that were soon to lose …ir hold. Orcagna, the possible author of the fresco of …a, died about the year 1376, as is proved by a document … existing, handing over the care of his two daughters, …ssa and Romola, to Cristofano Ristori, and with him it may … said that the greatest of the followers of the Giottesque tradition, in its best features of breadth and simplicity, h perished.

Antonio Veneziano, indeed, continues that tradition in so respects, and "thus forms an important link in the ch " which unites Orcagna to Masolino, Angelico and Masac(" Through him we may trace the passage from the art of t " 14th century to that which, taking a newer garb, beca " in the 15th century that of form."

His work in the Campo Santo of Pisa, illustrating the of S. Raineri is of importance, and it has been suggested Messrs. Crowe and Cavalcaselle that to his hand may due the frescoes in the Capellone dei Spagnuoli in S. Ma Novella.

But we find, indeed, during these last years of the 1 century, a lull in artistic development which is in contr with the splendid outburst which marked its beginning ; : it is during this lull that sculpture—which, though alwa subordinate in Italy to painting, is also always earlier in development—again comes to the front, and in the work such craftsmen as Ghiberti, Donatello, and the Della Robl takes awhile the lead of her sister art.

CHAPTER II.

THE CRAFTSMEN IN METAL AND MARBLE.

Lorenzo di Cione Ghiberti, a Florentine by birth, had been Lorenzo
)ught up by his father to the goldsmiths' trade—that trade Ghiberti,
iich had schooled many of the best Florentine craftsmen. 1378-1455.
his leisure he spent much of his time in modelling portraits
l casting for his friends imitations of antique gems and
ns, while at the same time he studied the art of painting.
is training no doubt influenced his later style, which was
tinguished for its delicacy and smoothness of technique, and
iich was at the same time so essentially pictorial that he
s been called by one critic "a painter in bronze." He
s at Rimini, occupied in decorating the palace of Carlo
itatesta, when his stepfather recalled him to Florence to
npete for the bronze gates of the Baptistery, and it was
 these he was destined to devote the most of his life,
iring in the friendship of Donatello and Brunelleschi, and
that marvellous world of Florentine culture, working at
spective, at goldsmiths' work (e.g., the splendid mitres of
pes Martin V. and Eugenius IV.), and writing also on Art
l Architecture (e.g., his "Treatise on Architecture"), in
iich last branch of art he was united for six years—very
ffectually—with Brunelleschi, who resented his superin-
idence of the work of the Duomo; and, lastly, in later life
ding high office as magistrate of his native town.
His great achievement are these gates of the Florentine Examples.
ptistery, which no less a judge than Michael Angelo was to
lare worthy of guarding the entrance to Paradise; in the
npetition for the designing of these gates, in the second
ir of the 15th century, there appeared as competitors with
iberti both Giacomo della Quercia of Siena, and Filippo
anelleschi, though this latter withdrew later from the
test.

Giacomo della Quercia, 1374-1438.

Della Quercia was certainly a formidable rival, and, Symonds suggests, "had the gates of the Baptistery be "entrusted to his execution we might have had a masterpi "of more heroic style." His genius had seemed to revive dying traditions of Sienese sculpture, of such craftsmen Lorenzo Maitani, who built the great cathedral of Orvi (1290-1330) and planned its wonderful façade; as Agostinc Giovanni and Agnolo di Ventura (1284-1380),—who worl with Giovanni Pisano on the Duomo of Siena, and carved monument to Guido Tarlati, the warrior bishop of Arezzo the Duomo of that city; as Tino, who carved at Pisa tomb of the ill-fated Henry VII. (1315), and that parti of the Ghibelline monarch and strong realist in art, Maes Gano, to whom we owe the monument of Bishop Tommasc Andrea, at Casole, near Siena. Born at Siena, and son o goldsmith, Giacomo at nineteen was already coming into no when he was driven from home by one of the party strugg which make up the history of Siena, involved, indeed, at t moment in the schemes of Gian Galeazzo Visconti; and h lost to us till we find him 10 years later at Florence, c peting unsuccessfully against Ghiberti for the doors of Baptistery, and carving the "Madonna della Cistola" i mandorla supported by angels over one of the side doors of Florentine Duomo. Thence he wandered to Ferrara, while busy on commissions there, is appointed by the Sien to be the sculptor of their "Fonte Gaia" in the great piaz

In one of the crises of party conflict and religious revival to which this emotional town was subject, they had torn do that antique statue of Venus, the ornament of their fount on the suggestion of a purist councillor, that the presenc the fair heathen goddess had brought to them their mis tunes. To replace it, Giacomo, now called "della Fon created a masterpiece; his design was a three-cornered para of marble, divided into nine niches, containing Madonna, Seven Virtues, and the Creation of Man and his Flight f Eden; beneath, from the basin, rose strange marine creatu children, wolves, dolphins, from whose open mouths the " unt" poured its stream. Yet, while busy on this work, he as creating too that masterpiece of monumental sculpture, e tomb of Ilaria del Carretto, wife of the Lord of Lucca, hich Ruskin has praised in such choicely chosen words : She is lying on a simple couch with a hound at her feet. . . . The hair is bound up in a flat braid over the fair brow, the sweet and arched eyes are closed, the tenderness of the loving lips is set and quiet ; there is that about them which forbids breath ; something which is not death nor sleep, but the pure image of both." Yet Giacomo had not, a rule, the classic elegance and the reserve which marks e great Florentine craftsmen ; compare his "Creation of an" in the bas-reliefs (15 in number) of the doorway of the asilica of S. Petronius at Bologna,—his next and last great ork,—with the suave beauty of the naked Eve in Ghiberti's)orway. Yet what passion and robust energy in Giacomo's prising Woman, what slumbering Titan is his recumbent [an ! We feel that young Buonarroti, an exile in Bologna, ay well have studied that sculpture and elaborated from it ie most stupendous of his creations in the Sistine.

The trial pieces of Ghiberti and Brunelleschi are preserved the Bargello of Florence, and have as their subject the Sacrifice of Isaac " ; the faults of Brunelleschi's work, the ant of repose and unity of composition, are in contrast with ie calm and harmonious dignity of Ghiberti's bas-relief.

Lorenzo Ghiberti— *continued.*

And the same qualities are noticeable throughout the nished work on the Baptistery Gates, representing various enes of Bible history. What, indeed, could be more eautiful than his rendering of a subject which has been so ften treated in the story of Creation, where the figure of Eve lides naked from her sleeping husband's side, and rises, pheld by angels and responsive to the uttered word of the eity.

This subject, as I have mentioned, had been approached by iotto, and may be seen at a few paces from the Baptistery mong the sculptures at the base of his Campanile ; but in he Eve of Ghiberti we feel that already the breath of a new influence has come into his art, the breath of that antique to whose marvellous art Italy was already turning with del and enthusiasm. We know how deeply Lorenzo Ghiberti himself impressed by the influences of this classical revi⸱ his enthusiasm over the marble Hermaphrodite, discovere that time in a vineyard of S. Celso, and his remark of ano antique, "the touch only can discover its beauties, wl " escape the sense of sight in any light," show how de(he had drunk of the Greek beauty of plastic form, with however, sacrificing his own originality in art.

His studies in another direction, that of perspective, wl had just been opened up, led him perhaps to overstep limits of the highest sculpture, in loading his bas-reliefs ⸱ elaborate landscape and figures massed at varying distan yet the sense of harmony and of plastic beauty in his gate bronze redeems, and more than redeems, these slight def of treatment, and places them on the level of the higl classic art, within at least that magic circle where f(remains predominant.

The Renaissance is already in the air, and the stra beauty of its hope is swaying all men's minds; no sculj was more rugged, more ₘearnest in his realism, than Donat(Niccolo di Betti Bardi, called Donatello, yet in some of his w there dwells a beauty as fascinating, if not so exquisite, a: the figures of Ghiberti. He had been but a youth of sevent at the time of the competition for the Baptistery, yet alre: it is related that his opinion had been sought. In his l(life he brings an inestimable advantage to the service of . he preserves that strength of design that gave its last superiority to the Florentine school.

Most admirable among his works is that figure of Da which yet remains in bronze in the Bargello of Florer The young champion stands in the moment of victory w his right foot planted on the helmeted head of Golia grasping a long straight sword—life size, and all but nak with a helmet pressing down the locks that escape luxuriant curls. He symbolizes the Christian's triumph,

Donatello, 1386–1468.

Examples.

Donatello] DAVID VICTORIOUS OVER GOLIATH. [BARGELLO OF FLORENCE.

By Donatello] GATTAMELATA [BEFORE S. ANTONIO
THE CONDOTTIERE. OF PADUA.
(*Fotog. Salviati.*)

touched already, in his naked beauty, with the fascinating, a deeply drawn-in, memories of Hellenic grace. Nor in his draped figures is Donatello less to be admired; it is of these that Messrs. Crowe and Cavalcaselle have judiciously observed:—"His draperies are an evident proof that he possessed an invigorating spirit. Whilst Ghiberti did nothing more than continue the abuse of superfluous festooned garments, and often made a figure but a peg on which to hang a tunic; whilst, in this, the great author of the gates of S. Giovanni failed to maintain the simple maxims of Giotto and Orcagna, Donatello, mindful of the laws of sculpture, sought ever to remind the spectator that, beneath the cloth there moved and breathed a human body; and he carried out this necessary law of statuary by defining the under forms, and by a judicious use of girdle and belts, a method in which he was faithfully followed by Mantegna and Michael Angelo."

Hardly less excellent than the "David" is that figure of S. George, in which "every line is indicative of the cool resolve which assures triumph, every portion of his body full of a dominant thought," which lately stood in one of the niches in Or San Michele, and has now been transferred to the Bargello; beneath, a relief full of vigour and beauty shows the Christian champion riding against the dragon, while the kneeling maiden watches in prayer her rescuer's doom or triumph. Nor can I pass by, without a word of the highest praise, that wonderful profile of an angel's head, whose spirituality of expression even surpasses, in our thoughts, the marvellous mastery of its technique, while, in a great equestrian statue of Gattamelata, for the city of Padua, he has left one of the noblest mounted portraits that the Renaissance produced.

In his work on the monuments of Pope John XXIII., of Cardinal Brancacci, and of Bartolommeo Aragazzi, Donatello was assisted by the Florentine sculptor Michelozzo Michelozzi, (architect for Cosimo dei Medici, of the Palazzo Medici (later Riccardi), of the villas of Careggi and Caffagiolo,

Michelozzo Michelozzi, 1396–1478.

of the Palazzo Vismara at Milan, and the Convent
S. Marco. The Cardinal had been a warm supporter of P
John in his many vicissitudes, and his tomb, a masterpi
of Donatello's monumental work, stands in the Church
Sant Angelo a Nilo at Naples, where he was buried in 14
Less fortunate was Aragazzi, the secretary of Pope Martin
a typical humanist, eminent for his vanity as for his learn
and poetry, since his monument in the church of his na
Montepulciano, which he hoped was to make his mem
eternal, was broken up, and exists only in beautiful fragme
One doorway alone remains, carved in Donatello's man

Antonio Averulino, called Filarete, died at Rome, 1450.

of the splendid Palazza Vismara, of which Filarete
written in his fanciful MS. upon architecture, wherein
had described the ideal city, with, in its centre, a g
cathedral—another S. Marco of Venice—"like the ideal n
durable, beautiful, and useful." In the same mingling s
of Paganism and Christendom Filarete modelled, for F
Eugenius, the great bronze gates of S. Peter's at R
(1431–43), assisted by a certain Simone, called also Donat
and thought it no violation of propriety to mingle v
Madonna and the Christ, with the martyrdom of S. P
and the great council held by Eugenius IV. at Flore
such subjects as his own frolics in the country, with a dor
laden with good things to eat, or such pure heathenism as
loves of Leda and the Swan, as the story of Jupiter
Ganymede. It was already the age of Humanism, the
when men turned passionately to this present world ; w
they worshipped Culture, as a lover adores his loved c
when they sought to hand down their memories and c
their very features in bronze or marble, in monumental w
of art. It was at such a time that that widely human gen
Leo Battista Alberti, could build for Sigismondo Panc
Malatesta (1447) that Temple of S. Francesco of Ri
which has been called " the most successful imitation of
antique ever accomplished " ; and entwining the joint ini
of Sigismondo and his mistress, the fair Isotta degli
adding medallions, bas-reliefs, inscriptions in Greek and L

ι sarcophagi wherein the eminent of Rimini were buried, e it almost a temple of the new Humanism, more like, ed, " a Pagan temple than a Christian church."

ι this strange memorial church Simone Donatello's hand aced in the sculptures, but among the best leaders of the culture, in its artistic side, stand out such Florentines Michelozzo and Donatello, both friends of Cosimo de ici, and the latter especially an earnest lover of nature of beauty of form.

have mentioned here what are unquestionably among his *Donatello—* .est efforts, while elsewhere his intense striving for *continued.* sm produced results which are less admirable.

ι a certain sense this is good, and as Mr. Symonds remarks, eeds indeed from the uncompromising candour of his art. a Magdalen were demanded from him he would not condescend to model a Venus and then place a book and skull on a rock beside her; nor did he imagine that the bloom d beauty of a laughing Faun were fitting attributes for a preacher of repentance. It remained for later artists, oxicated with antique loveliness and corroded with rldly scepticism, to reproduce the outward semblance Greek deities under the pretence of setting forth the ths of Christianity. Such compromise had not occurred Donatello."

t this realism is indeed perhaps carried too far in such s as that emaciated and repellent Magdalen of the ntine Baptistery, in which Donatello worked out "his a of a woman who had long lived upon the coarsest and ntiest food, and snatched weary slumbers upon the hard k that served her as a place of penitence and prayer."

know, too, Brunelleschi's candid criticism of a figure of t which Donatello had shown him. "You have crucified ic!" he had observed; and, indeed in their efforts to the structure of the body the artists of this period were apt to copy too faithfully their model's defects.

c

34   THE CRAFTSMEN IN METAL AND MARBLE.

Luca della Robbia, 1400-83.

Examples.

Andrea della Robbia, 1437-1528.

A more spiritual beauty, and at least more directly relig[ious] in its sentiment, dwells in the work of his contemporary, L[uca] della Robbia, whose life embraced the first 80 years of [the] 15th century.

Apprenticed in his youth to a goldsmith, it was not til[l he] had reached maturity in his art that he produced those gr[oups] of dancing children and choristers which still delight us in [the] Opera del Duomo; restraining himself in his terra-cotta w[ork] to the simplest effects of colour, to pure white on pale [blue] he has produced within those limits results which [are] incomparably exquisite in their utterance of expression.

His work, indeed, is emotional in the sweetest, and yet [in a] very subtlest way; like the still, sunlit quietness of [a] Tuscan morning of spring-time, even so the radiance of [a] happy Christian soul seems to dwell in the sweet profil[e of] his Madonnas.

Among his work we might, indeed, include those deli[cate] figures of children, naked, or sometimes yet wrapped in [the] swaddling clothes, which adorn the Hospital of the Inno[cents] in the Piazza dell' Annunziata of Florence, though thes[e are] more probably to be attributed to Luca's nephew, A[ndrea] della Robbia; but, indeed, Andrea, as well as Luca's four [sons] Giovanni, Luca, Ambrogio, and Girolamo, continued o[r] follow out his tradition, and were themselves imbued wit[h the] delicate fancy of his style.

The beautiful work which these craftsmen scattered th[rough] Florence, and through the churches too and conven[ts of] the hillsides of Tuscany, yet remain to the lover of [their] style for a wonder and delight; one might mention [that at] Pistoja (Ospedale del Ceppo), which took Andrea and h[is son] Luca II. eleven years of labour, La Verna, and those figu[res of] saints and angels which the Government has lately h[ad the] good sense to restore to the Certosa of the Val d'Ema, w[ithout] having exhausted the list.

I should mention, too, here Luca's work in marble bas[-relief] on the Campanile of the Florentine Duomo, where the [

By Agostino ai Duccio] GROUP OF ANGELS. [S. BERNARDINO OF PERUGIA. *(Fotog. Anderson.)*

Grammar, Astronomy, Geometry, and others were carried by him before 1445 ; and I would add that his later owers, in introducing into their work more varied and ser colours, departed, often to their own loss, from the raint and sweet simplicity of their teacher's work, though secret of his glaze was kept in his family, and has ppeared with them.

f interest in the terra-cotta sculpture of this period is the Agostino di k of Agostino di Gucci or di Duccio, who made the Duccio, after 1461. reliefs of Modena Cathedral (Life of S. Gimighano), and Examples. gned the beautiful façade of the oratory of S. Bernardino erugia, handling his terra-cotta somewhat in the manner onatello's flat-relief, yet aiming at more richness of detail, passion, than Luca's reserve would have permitted.

nd here, too, I may take the work of Mino da Fiesole and Mino da contemporaries, Antonio Rossellino, Matteo Civitali, and Fiesole, 1431-84. detto da Majano, all a little later than Luca della bia's time. The work of all these sculptors in marble, ly in relief, possesses similar characteristics, and is dis-ished by purity of design and a certain tranquility of ment. "To charge them with insipidity, immaturity, d monotony would be to mistake the force of genius played by them. We should rather assume that they ifined themselves to certain types of tranquil beauty, thout caring to realise more obviously striking effects, l that this was their way of meeting the requirements of lpture considered as a Christian art.

'he melody of their design, meanwhile, is like the purest music of Pergolese or Salvator Rosa, unapproachably t in simple outline, and inexhaustibly refreshing."

Mino's work the finish of the marble in its delicacy is Examples. pushed to the verge of insipidity, yet without reaching defect. In the tombs of the Badia (Count Ugo, and rdo Giugni the Gonfaloniere) at Florence, in the pulpit Duomo of Prato, and the altars in the Baglioni Chapel Pietro Cassinense at Perugia, in S. Ambrogio at Florence,

36   THE CRAFTSMEN IN METAL AND MARBLE.

and in the Cathedral of Fiesole (the beautiful tomb of Bish Salutati) may be seen some of his best work ; and I m mention also the profiles in low relief (Frederic, Duke Urbino, and Battista and Galeazzo Sforza) in the Barge Museum at Florence, while his great work in Rome, the to of the handsome and vain Pietro Barbo (Paul II.) exists o in fragments.

Antonio Rossellino, 1427 to about 1478. Examples.

A beautiful work by Rossellino is the monument to young Cardinal di Portogallo in the church of San Miniato Florence. The young prelate had been celebrated for beauty as well as his virtues, and we are told by his biograp that the resemblance has been preserved in this statue. H he is shown us as a most beautiful young man, lying, wrap in "the slumber that is death," and watched by ang beneath a curtained canopy.

The Rosellini were, indeed—like the Orcagnas, the Po juolos, the Robbias—a family of artists, and included f sculptors, of whom Bernardo was the architect of Nicholas and Pius II., and carved also the beautiful monument Lionardo Bruni, the scholar and poet, in Santa Croce Florence, while Antonio, of whom we are treating, was of the best sculptors of his day.

Rossellino's work at Monte Oliveto of Naples (especi the bas-relief of the Nativity) must also be mentioned ; wh it is in Lucca rather than in his work at Genoa (chapel S. John Baptist in Duomo) that we find some of the m interesting of Matteo Civitali's sculpture.

Matteo Civitali, 1435– 1501. Examples.

He had been chosen to adorn the Cathedral of this native city ; and here he designed in 1472 the marble mo ment of Pietro Noceto, Papal Secretary to Nicholas V., later that of Count Domenico Bertini (a noble Lucchese), adoring angels in the Capella del Sagramento, and the m beautiful chapel of the Santo Volto, "a gem of the pu "Renaissance architecture."

His work in this cathedral is full of beauty and devotio feeling, and repays a special study in this spot, whicl

THE CRAFTSMEN IN METAL AND MARBLE. 37

ned too by that most beautiful tomb of Ilaria del Caretto, uted in 1413 by Jacopo della Quercia; and of Matteo it ep, prayerful, intense feeling, as though the artist's soul, ured forth in ecstasy and adoration, had been given to e marble."

Jacopo della Quercia, 1374–1438.

here are two other artists to be yet enumerated among group of Italian sculptors whom I have just mentioned. derio di Settignano, a scholar of Donatello's, " il bravo esider, si dolce e bello," as Giov. Santi called him, has a masterpiece in his profusely decorated tomb of Carlo suppini, the famous humanist and Papal Secretary, in a Croce. At Florence, too, in the Palazzo Strozzi, his of Marietta di Palla degli Strozzi, treated with wonderful acy of technique and grasp of character, and "breathing e very spirit of urbanity," places his work in portraiture level with that of Mino.

Desiderio di Settignano, 1428–64.

t S. Gimignano, in his carvings of the altars of S. Fino mo) and S. Bartolo (S. Agostino), Benedetto da Majano rs that he had studied Ghirlandajo's frescoes, and owed aps even more to them than to the influence of Ghiberti chitectural backgrounds.

Benedetto da Majano, 1442–97.

e had begun life, we are told, as a *tarsiatore*, or worker rood mosaic—like his brother Giuliano, also an architect sculptor—and the influence of this training in his pic- l style in bas-relief is seen in his work in the pulpit of roce, Florence, at Faenza (in the beautiful and elaborate umental altar of S. Savino, in the Duomo), and in Monte eto at Naples.

architecture, indeed, he has left behind him a masterpiece, sternly splendid Strozzi Palace, which still frowns upon i its fierce strength in the Via Tornabuoni of Florence; was commissioned too by Filippo Strozzi to carve his ument, which stands in the Strozzi Chapel of S. Maria ella.

is to be transferred to a different school in treatment and ntiment to him, to turn to the work of northern Italy in

Antonio Amadeo, 1447? to about 1520. Andrea Fusina.

sculpture, to the mediæval tombs of the Scaligers at Vero to the terra-cotta modelling of Lombardy, to the work in great Certosa of Pavia, where Antonio Amadeo and Fusi together with the painter Ambrogio Borgognone, were work on that great monastery whose rich and comp beauty is still a monument to us of the restless striving the Renaissance.

In all this work the genius of the early Renaissance mal itself felt in its marvellous richness and complexity, nor (even the great work of the next century ever equal the dair reserve of Mino di Giovanni's marbles, the heavenly sweetn of the Robbia's pure white virgins. The work of this epc remains, too, pre-eminently Tuscan in its inception, a generally in its workmanship; even in these fanciful reli of S. Francesco of Rimini, the hands of two Florentines Ciuffagni and Simone da Donatello—are to be traced ; ev the palace of Duke Frederick at Urbino was continued the Florentine Pontelli, and Ambrogino da Milano—to whc we owe the dainty reliefs of dancing Cupids with gilded h and wings—may well have learnt his art in Tuscany ere l came to Urbino. Yet if Florence is pre-eminent, the inc viduality of Italian culture, of local influence, elsewhe asserts itself. In the tombs of the Doges at Venice, whe whole families like the Lombardi worked at sculpture a brought into their work a certain sumptuous richness, the mounted warriors that guard the tombs of the Scalige at Verona, in the terra-cotta work of Lombardy, with i feeling for sensuous beauty—such as we see in the Sac Monte of Varallo, in the work of Guido, called il Modanin at Monte Oliveto of Naples—or, again, in the fragile beau of the marble Medea (the work of Amadeo's hand) in tl Colleoni Chapel at Bergamo, we find again all that freshne and charm which fascinates in the work of the craftsmen Tuscany in metal and in marble, but expressed with tl variety, with the rich breath of personality, which vivifi the Italian race in that wonderful age of revival.

And already in our analysis of sculpture we stand on tb threshold of that great epoch where the form of Micha

;elo is to tower into significance as the master of a new
;age, that is to change the delicate grace of the past
something more terrible and more sublime.
he air is alive with new ideas, new hopes, new strivings.
us go back and inquire how painting, catching in her
fingers the torch from her sister art, had followed out
evolution of the Italian genius, and expressed in those
er days the effort of the yet uncertain future.

CHAPTER III.

PAINTERS OF EARTH AND OF HEAVEN.

While we resume then here our account of the advance Italian painting in those years which mark the commencen of the 15th century, we have at the onset to fix our read attention on a divergence in the aims which now occuj the artists' minds from what had sufficed an earlier age.

Those conceptions which filled the art of Giotto, wh he depicted with such vital force and "succeeded in presen " the idea, the feeling, the pith of the event, and piercer " once to the very ground-root of imagination," no lor filled to completeness the minds of a later age. Paintin very occupied now with completing the technicalities of craft ; in Florence and elsewhere she borrows from the g smith and the bronze-worker, in the clearness and precis of her detail. She is busy with the laws of perspective foreshortening ; and the details of nature, the very birds, beasts and flowers, attract her on every side ; she hears mighty echo of the antique world, and hearing it, she feel a sudden the fetters of mediæval monasticism loosen at her, she makes "the great discovery that the body of a ma " a miracle of beauty, each limb a divine wonder, each mu " a joy as great as sight of stars or flowers."

Mr. Monkhouse has well observed of these craftsmer the new epoch, that "their progress was not only technic " they indeed studied anatomy and perspective, and m " great improvements in composition, in drawing, and " colouring, but they also greatly extended the domain of " art with regard to subject, made a very great advance " landscape and portrait, and taught painting to reflect " life and thought of the day in spite of the restriction " their generally religious themes. . . . What they " was nothing more nor less than the construction of a and lovely language to express the whole emotions of humanity. The old language upon which theirs was based was only capable of expressing one limited class of feeling, a religious feeling certainly, but only a limited class of that, strictly confined to man's hopes and fears of the future state, as instigated by dogmas of the Church. They made this restricted language almost as universal as words, showing its capacity to express every joy and every sorrow, every feeling and every thought to which the mind, body, and soul of man is sensitive."

In following the work of the craftsmen of this epoch, of [such] men as Paolo Uccello, the Pollajuoli, later even in a Lippo himself or the greater Masaccio, we shall see the working out of these tendencies, always sincere in their feeling, often exaggerated in their expression; what new impulse, indeed, has not sometimes overstrained in the insistence of its first appeal? *Paolo Uccello 1397–1475.*

Paolo Doni nicknamed Uccello from his love of painting birds, had been apprenticed in youth to Lorenzo Ghiberti, "garzone di bottega."

Hence came, perhaps, his tendency to sharpness of outline, and passion for perspective; of the four panels of battle scenes by his hand, once adorning the gardens of the Bartolini at Gualfonda, one only is in Florence, in the Gallery of the Uffizi, another in the Louvre, while another is in the National Gallery of London.

Messrs. Crowe and Cavalcaselle have observed that "a daring boldness of action marks the knights and barded steeds at tilt, which form the subject of the panel at Florence: perspective of broken lances, shields and helmets, is laboriously carried out . . . . but the spectator has before him the lifeless and wooden models of divers figures, their geometrical substance without the final dressing that should give life to the form and its action."

The same remarks might apply to the panel in the National Gallery, representing the Battle of S. Egidio, in which

Malatesta and his young nephew Galeazzo were t[o] prisoners.

In the foreground we see Carlo Malatesta giving command to charge, mounted on a white horse, and cla[d] steel, with turban of crimson and gold ; behind him his neph[ew] a beautiful, fair-haired boy, carries his visor in his r[ight] hand, his knights advance behind, and the trumpeters [with] their long clarions peal out the charge. The elabo[rate] perspective in the background is occupied with figure[s] crossbow-men and spearmen ; we cannot fail to notice [the] wooden character of the horses depicted. But the points [we] have to dwell most on here, as especially characteristic [of] Uccello, are the efforts shown in this painting at perspect[ive] at detail, and naturalistic treatment ; an example of laboured treatment of foreshortening is in the figure of [a] knight or man-at-arms lying on his face with his b[ack] towards the spectator.

What we have said will give some idea of Uccel[lo's] peculiar style, which is quite as marked in the frescoes [of] his hand in the cloisters of S. Maria Novella, giving sce[nes] from the Old Testament, the Creation, Deluge, and Sacrifice of Noah.

He painted too, about 1436, for the Signoría, a port[rait] of the English Condottière, Hawkwood, in the Floren[t] Duomo ; the painting did not give satisfaction, and he [was] ordered to repaint it in terra verde, or dead colour. Vasa[ri's] account of Uccello would give the impression of a man devo[ted] to his craft, studying much, producing little, and earn[ing] little ; we get, too, in this account, the story of his fli[ght] from the monks of S. Miniato, who had fed him exclusiv[ely] on cheese.

He was perhaps acquainted with Masaccio and lived at least his seventy-third year, having visited Urbino wh[en] seventy-two, where Messrs. Crowe and Cavalcaselle find str[ong] traces of his style in a *predella* in S. Agatha, long attribu[ted] to Giusto of Ghent.

He seems to have died in poverty, and was buried in Maria Novella of Florence.

Along with Uccello, with whom he was united in friendship, Dello Delli (about 1404–64). ...y be mentioned here the artist Daniello or Dello Delli. ...ke his friend Paolo Doni, he commenced by the study of ...lpture, but gaining a great reputation as a painter of ...dding chests, or "Cassone," he devoted himself to this ...nch of art. Political troubles led him to fly from Florence ... Siena in 1424, thence to Venice (about 1427), and finally ... Spain, where he lived in the service of the Kings of ...agon and attained knighthood. He is said to have been ...mitted to return to Florence in 1446, and to have painted, ...sari tells us, in the cloisters of S. Maria Novella with ...cello. He died, however, in Spain in 1464.

And here, before continuing our narrative, it may be of ... to the reader to review briefly the classification of the late ...on Rumohr, quoted with approval by Signor Morelli in his ...k on the Berlin Gallery, though he leaves out the interest- ...artist with whom we have next but one been immediately ...cerned. In this view the predominating naturalism of the ...rentines branched out in two opposite directions; action, ...ement, the expression of intense and strong passions, ...me the inheritance of the school of Fra Filippo (Masolino ...anicale, Masaccio, Fra Filippo Lippi, Francesco Pesellino, ...dro Botticelli, Filippino Lippi); realistic probability, and ...ectness in hitting off the characteristics of individual ...gs, was the aim of a school which began with Cosimo ...elli, although it shot far ahead of his latest achievement ...sso Baldovinetti, Gozzoli, Roselli, Domenico Ghirlandajo, ...his brother-in-law Mainardi), while a third division of ...Florentine School was directly produced by the efforts of ...tors (Lorenzo Ghiberti, Antonio and Piero Pollajuolo, ...rea Verrocchio and others). In this classification, which it ...ell to have in view without necessarily following it closely, ...ames have been added by Morelli to Rumohr's general

PAINTERS OF EARTH AND OF HEAVEN.

The Pollajuoli.
Antonio Pollajuolo, 1429–98.
Piero Pollajuolo, 1441–89.

The realism of Uccello's art, its sculpture-like precision close study of detail and perspective, are reproduced in work of his contemporaries Antonio and Piero Pollaju Antonio had been apprenticed to his father Jacopo, who perhaps worked under Ghiberti, and himself opened a g smith's shop, where he was joined later by his brother P They are a good example of the strong influence of sculpt work on the painting of the epoch. " Painting being car
" on in the goldsmith's shop, was subjected to so muc
" these rules as might be properly applied ; and pictures c
" to resemble, in colour and other features, imitations of si
" and bronze works."

" The Pollajuoli, Verrochio, Botticelli, and even Dome Ghirlandajo were the exponents of this new fashion."

Antonio Pollajuolo was indeed one of the most fam goldsmiths of his time, and has had the highest praise f that master of his craft, Benvenuto Cellini.

In every branch of the goldsmith's art, for which Flor was then so famous, his craftsmanship was shown. designed, and often carried out himself, church ornam basins, helmets, chains, and " crucifixes of the most s workmanship." His bas-reliefs are equally excellent, show a vigour of conception and of modelling equal to Dona himself ; there is a crucifixion in the Bargello of Florenc which the Magdalen tears out her long locks in a sple frenzy of grief—the spirit of some Greek Bacchante pene ing within the Christian forms—where, though it is attributed to him, I have often fancied to myself the t of this master ; and not less remarkable for its murd enthusiasm, its intensity of "frozen passion," is his celeb engraving of ten naked men fighting duels in a wood. their pictorial efforts the two Pollajuoli must be t together, as men whose style was affected by their contin labours in plastic art, and mainly in works of bronze silver.

Piero had worked under Andrea del Castagno, and in their paintings he represents, perhaps, most of the pictorial element derived from his teacher, while Antonio is rather the sculptor and student of the antique, attempting a new medium. A good example of this is in the small paintings of the Uffizi, representing the encounters of Hercules with Antaeus and with the Hydra; as also in the Virtues, originally painted for the Mercatanzia of Florence, one of which, the Prudence, is in the Uffizi; the S. Sebastian of the Pitti Gallery; and, lastly, the large S. Sebastian of the National Gallery, the masterpiece, Vasari's mind, of this artist.

Examples.

In visiting the last painting we have noticed especially the careful detail, the naturalism of treatment (and here we should point to the archer stooping to bend his cross-bow), the classic accessories, the vigour and intensity of expression; the careful modelling, too, of the nude, and the reddish flesh tones, are usually characteristic of these artists.

The Roman arch in the background shows already the influence of classic memories, but indeed, as Mr. Monkhouse observes, supremely dominant in the whole work is "the revived interest in the figure of man for its own sake—not, or at least not only, as a means of spiritual expression, as with Fra Angelico, and his forerunners; not yet as the standard of beauty, as with the sculptors of Greece, or the masters of the 16th century, but as a miracle of organised structure, a machine of unrivalled complexity and economy, of suppleness and strength, Protean in its contours, inexhaustible in its ever-shifting play of curves and angles, infinite in its indication of feeling."

Andrea del Castagno must be mentioned along with the Pollajuoli as "the leaders of this branch of realism, due to admiration for the newly studied mechanism of the human form. They seemed to have cared but little to select their types or to accentuate expression, so long as they were able to portray the man before them with fidelity. The comeliness of average humanity was enough for them. The difficulties

Andrea del Castagno, 1396–1457.

"of reproducing what they saw exhausted their force..
"while only here and there, in minor paintings for the]
"part, the poet that was within them saw the light."

Andrea Verrochio (b. 1435, d. 1488).

And to be mentioned appropriately here in connection ·
the Pollajuoli is the gifted Florentine, Andrea del Verroc
Vasari had described him as "a goldsmith, a teacher of
"spective, a sculptor and carver, a painter, and a musici
(Vol. V., p. 139); and if he resembles Leonardo in
complex abundance of talents, he is like his pupil too in
fact that but little of his painting (one genuine work o
survives, and that his influence over others was greater {
his own actual production in art. As Crowe observes, '
"productions of Leonardo, as well as of Lorenzo di C
"teach us to appreciate at their just value the attainmer
"their master, whose complex of work is confined to a
"remarkable examples"; and he illustrates this fact by
remarkable similarity between the drawings of Verroc
Leonardo, and Lorenzo, the style (which is Verrocl
originally) being the same. Taking his work in sculp
first, we have the bronze of the youthful David, still
Florence, which certainly, as Symonds says, "outdoes
hardest work of Donatello by its realism." The attitud
free, the right hand wields the sword; a cuirass, a hip-cl
and greaves cover the lean figure in which the artist sho
his careful study of nature and anatomy. But most charm
to my mind, is the "Boy and Dolphin," formerly at Care
now in the courtyard of the old Palazzo at Florence
fluttering caprice, if you will, but so dainty, so full of ;
movement, that he scarcely seems of bronze, this "put
whose round, fat limbs Lorenzo loved to reproduce, who sque
the water from the mouth of the struggling fish. In 1
Verrochio finished the bronze of S. Thomas Searching out
Wounds of Christ, for one of the niches of Or San Michel
Florence; and in 1488 he died at Venice, leaving behind
the model of the noble equestrian statue of the Condott
Colleoni, which was completed subsequently by Leopardi.
the conception of this great work, the finest equestrian st

STATUE OF THE CONDOTTIERE COLLEONI. (VENICE.)

BY ANDREA VERROCHIO (COMPLETED BY LEOPARDI).

(See p. 46.)

the Renaissance, he had almost certainly been influenced by natello's "Gattamelata," still at Padua, facing S. Antonio; Crowe very justly observes, that "Donatello, in fact, shares vith Verrochio the honour of having, in equestrian statues, nade a nearer approach to the antique than any Italian culptor of subsequent or previous times." The great Contiere had left his wealth to Venice on condition his statue uld be placed in the Piazza di S. Marco; he still remains ore the Scuola di S. Marco, where he was placed by an enious quibble of the senators. His statue no doubt uenced Leonardo, Verrochio's pupil, when he came later to duce his own equestrian work. From Verrochio, too, he took type of face which became peculiar to himself and his ool. And in the "Baptism of Christ," by Verrochio, the st's sole surviving work in painting, the young Leonardo aid to have made his first essay, in the figure of the kneeling ;el nearest the spectator on the right of the canvas. There ertainly a contrast between the tender grace, the bewitching uty of feature in the figure, and the bony realism of rrochio's Saviour or the unfinished S. John. This work is he Accademia of Florence. The beautiful " Virgin adoring Infant Christ," of the National Gallery, once assigned Ghirlandajo, shows much of the influence of Verrochio. we has suggested that it is not impossible that this panel uld have been executed by da Credi in Verrochio's atelier; ertainly shows his manner rather than that of the Polla-i, and, like the "Angel and Tobias" of the same collection, y one who had studied the goldsmith's art.

astagno was, as we have seen, the teacher of Piero lajuolo, and a contemporary of Uccello, a man of strong isive temperament. His best examples are the equestrian ure of Niccolo da Tolentino—which will bear comparison h Uccello's Hawkwood—and the frescoes of the Villa idolfini at Legnaia, the remains of which are now in the izi ; he has a small Crucifixion in the National Gallery. There is vigour and power in these figures of heroes and ils of the Pandolfini, among whom were Dante, Petrarch,

Andrea del Castagno— continued.

Boccaccio, Farinata, and Pippo Spano, the victor of
Turks, who defiantly bends the steel of his rapier within
hands.

Domenico
Veneziano;
worked from
1436-61.

Vasari has a story of Castagno's having waylaid
murdered at the street corner Domenico Veneziano, who
his rival in the frescoes he painted for the Hospital of S. Ma
Nuova at Florence; but it has been argued by Signor Gaet
Milanese that Domenico survived Andrea by four years,
latter having died of the plague in 1457.

Domenico was connected with the fortunes of the Med
family, and was possibly of Venetian origin.

He was certainly resident in Perugia, and probably ca
thence into Florence on the recommendation of the Medici,
paint the choir of S. Maria Nuova.

Examples.

He was acquainted with Fra Lippo and Fra Angelico,
his work—notably his picture in S. Lucia de' Bardi at Floret
now in the Uffizi—has a certain connection with these arti
though elsewhere Castagno's influence seemed to have touch
him.

Two heads of saints from his hand, vigorous but repaint
are in the National Gallery; and to him Morelli 'wo
ascribe the frescoes of SS. Francis and John Baptist—gi
formerly to Castagno—in S. Croce of Florence.

He appears to have settled in Florence, and died there
1461.

Piero della
Francesca;
1420?-1506?

Especially among the scientific painters of this period
progress must be placed Piero della Francesca, a native
Borgo San Sepolcro and a pupil of Domenico Veneziano.
studied thoroughly the principles of drawing and modelli
and composed in Italian a treatise on the new art of perspecti
which had so fascinated Uccello.

Born among the mountains of Umbria, his good fortune
him into early contact with Domenico Veneziano, by whom
was employed on the frescoes of S. Maria Nuova at Florenc

Mr. Monkhouse, after mentioning that his real name
Pietro di Benedetto dei Franceschi, that he probably stud
under Paolo Uccello, and that he learned to work in oils fr

nenico Veneziano, observes " In the feeling of his work he
is Umbrian, but technically and intellectually he belongs
rather to the scientific school of Florence—to the realists and
experimentalists of the fifteenth century." And he adds,
"a strange mixture of impulses makes his work unusually
interesting."
For while he entered into the study of nature with an ardour
equal to that of his master or of Del Castagno, whom he must
have known, while he adopted their style without a thought
of selection, but with the determination to master the true
laws of motion and life, he yet retains much of the Umbrian
spirituality and intensity of emotional power. " Those who
have once seen," says Mr. Symonds, " his fresco of the
Resurrection in the hall of the Compagnia della Misericordia
at Borgo San Sepolcro will never forget the deep impression
of solitude and aloofness from all earthly things produced by
it. It is not so much the admirable grouping and masterly
drawing of the four sleeping soldiers, or even the majestic type
of the Christ, emergent without effort from the grave, as the
communication of a mood felt by the painter and instilled into
our souls, that makes this by far the grandest, most poetic, and
most awe-inspiring picture of the Resurrection. . . . . Thus,
with Piero for mystagogue, we enter an inner shrine of deep
religious revelation."
To be mentioned with equal praise is his fresco of the
Dream of Constantine in S. Francesco at Arezzo, and his
portrait of Sigismondo Malatesta, Lord of Rimini, and
Federigo of Urbino; the latter of these portraits is in the
Gallery of the Uffizi. Of interest especially to the English
student will be the genuine picture of Piero now in the
National Gallery, representing the Baptism of Christ, and
which was formerly part of an altar-piece in the priory of
S. Giovanni Evangelista at Borgo S. Sepolcro, as well as a
Nativity in the same collection, unfinished, painted in oils, and
very original in treatment.

These paintings, too, are of special interest in the insight
they give us to Piero's method of oil painting, in which

D

he improved so much on his predecessors, especially in treatment of the flesh tints.

"The great laws of composition," it has been said of epoch of advance, "founded on the models of Giotto, "plastic element made dominant by the sculptors of the "century, the scientific perspective of lines, which owe "grand impulse to Uccello, the more subtle one of atmospl "which Masaccio mastered . . . . . were summe "in a great measure by Domenico Ghirlandajo." We notice here, too, that the change in the use and applicatic medium carried out by the Peselli, and enlarged and exte by the Pollajuoli, owed much to the example of one though not a Florentine, had formed himself on the pι Florentine models—the painter Piero della Francesca.

But the most noteworthy character in the epoch we l just traversed, in his immense influence on contemporary succeeding painters, is the Florentine Tommaso di Giovanni, called Masaccio.

Masolino da Panicale, 1384-1447. Examples.

He had studied with Masolino, who was born in S. C in 1384 and whose sole authentic works are probably frescoes at Castiglione di Olona near Milan, and those fres in S. Clement's of Rome which were till recently attribute Masaccio. They were executed for the Cardinal Br Castiglione, and show similar technique to the frescoe Olona above mentioned, while it should be added Masolino's hand may be traced also in three of the Bran Chapel frescoes which Masaccio continued.

Masaccio, 1402-29.

Masaccio was born at S. Giovanni, in the valley of Upper Arno in 1402.

"In his frescoes," says Mr. Symonds, "the qua "essential to the style of the Renaissance—what Vasari "the modern manner—appear precociously full formed . "In Masaccio's management of drapery we discern "influence of plastic art; without concealing the limbs, w "are always modelled with a freedom that suggests the p "of movement even in stationary attitudes, the volum "folds and broad masses of powerfully coloured rai vest his forms with a nobility unknown before in painting. [His] power of representing the nude is not less remarkable. [B]ut what above all else renders his style attractive is the [u]se of aerial space. For the first time in art the forms of [l]iving persons are shown moving in a transparent medium of [li]ght graduated to degrees of distance, and harmonised by [to]nes that indicate an atmospheric unity." These qualities Examples. [will] be best exemplified in the great frescoes of the Brancacci [Cha]pel in the Church of the Carmine at Florence, in which the [sens]e of atmosphere and of what has been called "tactile [valu]es"* has been so wonderfully realised, and which soon [beca]me "the school where all succeeding artists studied, and [whe]nce Raphael deigned to borrow the composition and the [fig]ures of a portion of his cartoons."

[On] the importance, therefore, of these frescoes in the [evol]ution of Florentine painting it is impossible to insist too [stron]gly; they represent the Fall and Expulsion from Paradise, [prob]ably the first in order of time of the scenes painted, and [the s]tory of S. Peter, in eight frescoes, in the last of which, [the R]esurrection of the Child, Filippino Lippi's hand has been [perh]aps at work.

[In] these frescoes the artist introduced many portraits, amongst [whic]h Vasari mentions those of Donatello, Masolino, his [broth]er, Antonio Brancacci, his patron, and others, and here [na]ture itself seems reflected on the eye of the spectator as he [see]s a number of heads in the same plane preserving their [pr]oper relative position and surrounded by atmosphere. . . [Th]e first years of the 15th century thus witnessed the [suc]cessful production of that harmony of colour, relief, and [sen]se of distance which entitled the painters of the so-called [go]lden age to the admiration of the world."

[Th]e frescoes in S. Clemente of Rome, in which [S. C]atherine appears before the Emperor Maxentius, have [been] more recently assigned to Masolino, and not Masaccio; [of th]e latter artist's easel pictures there are few remaining, the

---

* Appendix II.

D 2

two portraits in the Uffizi bearing his name being prob[ably]
by Lippi and Botticelli, but three small pictures in the B[rera]
Gallery (Adoration of the Magi and two other subjects) [may]
be classed as genuine, but not important, works by Masac[cio.]

A mystery hangs over this great artist's fate. He [left]
for Rome in 1429 and totally disappeared; at the ag[e of]
twenty-seven he was thus lost, but he had left the impres[s of]
his genius indelibly stamped upon his age.

One is tempted to remember the proud epitaph writter[n by]
Annibale Caro of this painter, and quoted by Giorgio Va[sari,]
which ends with the words: "*Master of all the res[t,]
learned of none myself.*"

From Masaccio we may pass on without a break in [the]
continuity of progress to the great masters of the [High]
Renaissance; but I would prefer to linger awhile with [one]
who remained untouched by the effort that was around t[hem,]
and yet have for later ages an inexhaustible charm.

"Tracing the history of Italian painting," it has [been]
said, "is like pursuing a journey down an ever broade[ning]
" river, whose affluents are Giotto and Masaccio, Ghirlan[dajo,]
" Signorelli, and Mantegna.

Fra Angelico, "We have to turn aside and land upon the shore in [a]
1387-1455. " to visit the heaven-reflecting lakelet, self-encompassed [and]
" selcuded, called Angelico." In the year 1407 "Br[other]
" Joannes Petri di Mugello of Vicchio, who excelled [as a]
" painter," made the first profession in the Conver[t of]
S. Domenico at Fiesole, being then 20 years of age. V[asari]
has painted his character in words which are full of feel[ing.]
" He was wont to say that the pursuit of art required res[t and]
" a life of holy thoughts; that he who inherited the a[rt of]
" Christ should be with Christ . . . . The saints v[which]
" he depicted had more of the air and semblance of saints[than]
" any produced by others. He never retouched or al[tered]
" anything that he had once finished, but left it as i[t]
" turned out, the will of God being that it should b[e.]
" Some go so far as to say that Fra Giovanni never [took]

By Fra Angelico

THE BLESSED IN PARADISE.
(DETAIL.)

ACADEMY OF FLORENCE.
(*Fotog. Alinari.*)

have touched a brush had he not first humbled himself in prayer." In these and similar traits we see proofs of a life wrapped up in the ardours of mysticity, a pious and sweet character absorbed in its deep religious conviction.

He takes from none, for his spirit is alien to the effort of contemporaries.

'While the artists around him were absorbed in mastering the laws of geometry and anatomy, Fra Angelico sought to express the inner life of the adoring soul .... His world is a strange one; a world not of hills and fields, and rivers and men of flesh and blood, but one where the people are embodied ecstacies, the colours tints from evening clouds or apocalyptic jewels, the scenery a flood of light or a background of illuminated gold. His mystic gardens, where the ransomed souls embrace and dance with angels on the lawns outside the City of the Lamb, are such as were never trodden by the foot of man in any paradise of earth." When I say, however, he takes from none, I allude more especially to the artists of his time.

In this respect he may be compared with one of his contemporaries, Gentile da Fabriano, a painter who shared nothing with such men as Uccello or Verocchio, though to his Umbrian pietism he unites a love of nature. {Gentile da Fabriano, about 1370 to about 1450.}

His masterpiece is the Adoration of the Magi in the Academia at Florence; the rich costume of the Eastern kings, their train of servants, their hawks and horses, are painted by him with singular fidelity; and nothing can be more true to nature than the wild flowers he has copied in the frame-work of the picture. The picture assigned to him in the Hotel Cluny at Paris, and dated 1408, is given by Crowe and Cavalcaselle to Don Lorenzo Monaco, a monk of the Camaldolese Order, who worked at Monte Oliveto at Florence in 1410, at the great Convent of the Angioli there, and also at Empoli. He drew his inspiration from the Gaddi, as Angelico, to a less extent, from Orcagna. {Examples. Lorenzo Monaco, worked about 1403-15. Examples.}

54   PAINTERS OF EARTH AND OF HEAVEN.

Fra Angelico—
continued.

"As the bee," it has been said of him, "hovers over
flowers and carries the honey to his hive, so Angelico dr
from Orcagna some of the sweets of his pencil, those pa1
in fact, which were suited to his artistic nutriment.
used Orcagna's types after purifying and idealizing them

And Cosmo Monkhouse, too, speaking of his "Ch1
with the Banner of the Redemption," that beautiful work
the National Gallery, says, "If we compare the predella w
Orcagna's 'Coronation of the Virgin' we shall find 1
artistic ideals very much the same. . . The chief dif
ence between the two works is this, that Fra Angelico
carried expression to a perfection which was impossible
Orcagna."

Examples.

In the Convent of S. Domenico at Fiesole it was t
Fra Giovanni completed some of his earliest work ; for it
from here that the French took the beautiful "Corona1
of the Virgin" now in the Louvre ; but even better kn(
are those frescoes of the Convent of S. Marco at Flore1
which was rebuilt by Michelozzo Michelozzi between 1
and 1441.

Here in 1438 Angelico painted the altar-piece of
choir, representing the Virgin enthroned, and in the y(
following covered the walls of the convent—even each l1
separate cell—with those frescoes which are the n
exquisite expression of his genius.

Here the Virgin listens to the message of Gab
swooping down before her like some great bird with rust
plumes ; here the Saviour bends his head upon the cros
perfect resignation—in all the deep religious feeling of
man finds a true and fitting expression.

To visit these frescoes is to enter within a world of i1
sentiment, to hear the music of the hidden lutes of hea1
and be wafted awhile, if the mood be only ours, within
veil of that ecstatic dream.

At S. Marco Fra Angelico may have met, in 1442,
Pope Eugenius IV., and, as the story goes, was offered

n the Archbishopric of Florence, which he declined in
our of his brother Antonino, "a man erudite," so he said,
ble, and fearing God."
Eugenius died in 1447 and his successor, Nicholas V.,
ught Angelico from Orvieto, where he was at work on a
st Judgment in the Duomo, for the second time to Rome,
ere he decorated the Chapel of the Vatican, which bears
it Pope's name, with scenes from the lives of S. Stephen
1 S. Lawrence.
He died in Rome at the age of 68, and was buried in the
irch of the Minerva, where in his epitaph we read these
rds, " Some works are for Earth, others for Heaven." He
no successor to his style, for Benozzo Gozzoli, " the
upil of Fra Angelico, but in no sense the continuator of his
radition, exhibits the blending of several styles by a genius
of less creative than assimilative force." Leaving Rome in
19, Benozzo stayed for some time in Montefalco, where
found employment; but his best work was done at
Gemignano, where he decorated the whole choir of the
irch of S. Agostino with scenes from the life of that saint,
the Capella Riccardi at Florence, and the Campo Santo
Pisa. In the frescoes of the Capella Riccardi, in those
nes of the Nativity where "his fancy supplied him with
nultitudes of angels waving rainbow coloured wings above
air mortal faces," Benozzo has always seemed to me at his
t; more important indeed, perhaps, are the frescoes of Pisa,
resenting scenes from the Old Testament history, com-
iced in 1469—when he first touched the fresco of Noah
his family, which is one of his best—and finished in 1485,
s occupying sixteen years. In the fresco of the Tower
Babel there are portraits of the Medici, with the scholars
ino and Politiano. To be noticed also is his quaint little
el, possibly part of a "Cassone," representing the
ape of Helen," in the National Gallery, of which
. Monkhouse observes that it is the first in which the
ist has entered the romantic world of classic legend, and,.

Benozzi Gozzoli, 1420-98.

with one exception, the first which is purely secular i
subject. He loves to introduce also rich architectural detail
quaint birds or beasts, and touches of common life ; " he fe
" an enjoyment like that of Gentile da Fabriano in depictin
" the pomp and circumstance of pageantry, and no Florentiu
" of the 15th century was more fond of assembling tl
" personages of contemporary history in groups." He seem
happy indeed in this "many coloured world of inexhaustib
delight," in which his fancy draws its inspiration, and h
indefatigable industry its object ; he can seldom touch tl
level of the great ones in Italian painting, but yet in his ow
limits he is often entirely delicious.

CHAPTER IV.

THE ENIGMA OF THE RENAISSANCE.

[If] Fra Angelico represents the reaction, the return to the [older] tradition of purely religious painting, we have seen that [the] reaction was only temporary.
[T]he spirit of the age was too strong to be repressed, the [love] of science and nature too intense to be kept within the [strict] limits of the cloister; even Benozzo, the heavenly [mas]ter's own pupil, turns from the vision of angel faces to [the] manifold delightsomeness of this living world, to the [plea]sure of its pageantry, the gladness and the humour of its [fami]liar everyday life. Yet the contrast, we might almost [say] the schism, existed, and was only deepened by the [grow]th of the new spirit of humanism, by the resurrection of [the c]ulture, the legends, and beliefs of the beautiful old heathen [world], which came to fill the minds of Florentine scholars and [artis]ts at this epoch. Personified as this new Culture was, in [the b]rilliant circle of poets, artists, philosophers, who surrounded [the] Medici, it pervaded the whole of Florentine intellectual [life], and deepened the division between the claims of the Church, [the] mistress of holy things, and the joy in this new-found [wor]ld of Life. In none does this schism of creed and [cond]uct appear more glaring than in the brilliant and [imag]inative painter I am about to mention.
[L]ike Benozzo, Fra Filippo Lippi was under the powerful [patr]onage of the Medici. He was left an orphan at an early [age], and was placed by his aunt in the convent of the Carmine [at F]lorence, being registered there in 1420. For monastic life [he s]eems to have had no natural vocation; his pleasure loving [and] yet richly endowed temperament caused scandal even in [an a]ge which was not certainly severe in morals. It has been

Fra Filippo Lippi, 1412?-69.

said of him with justice, that "it can scarely be doubted t
" the schism between his practice and profession served
" debase a genius of fine imaginative quality. . . . .
" Bound down to sacred subjects, he was too apt to m
" angels out of street urchins, and to paint the portraits of
" peasant loves for Virgins."

Mr. Monkhouse, too, dwelling on this "human qualit
in Fra Lippo's pictures in the National Gallery ("St. J(
Baptist and six other Saints" and an "Annunciatior
observes "The Annunciation is conceived in the same sp
" of tender and poetic realism. Robbed of his nimbus a
" wings, the announcing angel is only a comely, round-hea(
" Florentine boy, with closely curling hair, who delivers
" message with simple and charming grace, and she,
" Virgin, who receives it with so sweet and humble a courte
" might be his sister; but if the types are not very dis1
" guished, or the emotion greatly elevated, the whole c(
" position is lovely and harmonious." Morelli has noticed
Fra Filippo's work his hands—blamed even by his cont(
poraries, as Vasari relates—"stumpy, awkward, and ba
modelled," and his type of ear, "round and clumsy in f(
and usually curved inwards." In his colouring the prevai
tones are pale blue and pale grey, while "the landscap
" Fra Filippo, and of his pupil Francesco Pesellino, resem
" that of his contemporaries, and like Fra Angelico's cons
" principally either of a series of rounded hills, or of poi1
" rocks."*

Examples.   A good example of his earlier work is the Nativity in
Academy of Florence, where the Virgin kneels in pr
before the recumbent Jesus, a subject repeated in the beau1
picture of the Berlin Gallery; and in the same gallery
Florence is one of the best examples of his matured ger
The subject is a Coronation of the Virgin amongst angels
adoring figures of saints, many of whom are Bernardine mo1
and one, with the tonsure, to the right, is a half-ler

* See Appendix III.

By Fra Filippo Lippi] THE CORONATION OF THE VIRGIN (DETAIL). [ACADEMY OF FLORENCE. *(Fotog. Alinari.)*

portrait of Fra Filippo himself. An angel in front of him holds a scroll on which is written "Is perfecit opus." There is a quaintness of beauty in this painting which makes it one of the most attractive of the master's, and which has suggested some of the most charming lines in that poem in which Robert Browning has analysed with much subtlety of feeling the characteristics of this Florentine painter; even at a distance our memory recalls those figures of angels and adoring saints and grey-robed Bernardines, among whom the painter looks up, half proud and half bashful in that throng.

At Prato, near Florence, Fra Filippo was commissioned to paint the frescoes of the choir of the Cathedral Church, and here he seems to have fixed his abode in 1456. These frescoes, representing the story of S. John Baptist and S. Stephen are among the best of his work, and the scene of Salome dancing before Herod has been called his masterpiece.

"Her movement across the floor before the tyrant and his guests at table, the quaint fluttering of her drapery, the ill-bred admiration of the spectators, their horror when she is bringing the Baptist's head to Herodias, and the weak face of the half-remorseful Herod, are expressed with a dramatic power that shows the genius of a poet painter. And even more lovely than Salome are a pair of girls locked in each other's arms close by Herodias on the dais."

Morelli has described these frescoes of the Cathedral of Prato as Fra Lippo's greatest works; and he adds, "these splendid paintings were begun in 1456 and completed in 1464; they were therefore executed at the same period as Mantegna's equally celebrated frescoes in the Eremitani Chapel at Padua. In order to understand the aims and capacities of art at that date in its highest achievements these two great works should be studied and compared."

It was at Prato that, according to Vasari's story the friar saw the novice, Lucretia Buti, while painting a picture for the high altar of the Convent Chapel of Santa Margherita of Prato, and obtained permission from the nuns to take her as model for the figure of the Virgin.

60   THE ENIGMA OF THE RENAISSANCE.

"He could not resist the opportunity thus offered to hi
and after some wooing, he induced Lucretia to sacrifice hers
to him, and took her home. . . . . The sisters of Sa[n]
Margherita did their utmost to recover Lucretia, but with[o]
avail; and the fruit of this illicit intercourse was Filipp[o]
Lippi, a painter of some fame after the death of Fra Filipp[o]
(Crowe and Cavalcaselle).

Tradition has assigned a portrait of Lucretia to the Mado[n]
of Fra Filippo in the Pitti Gallery—"a circular pict[u]
"representing the half-length Virgin, seated in a chair w
"the Infant Saviour, all but naked, on her knee. . . T
"group of the Virgin and Child reminds us forcibly of th
"of Donatello or Desiderio da Settignano. The type of
"Virgin's head, like most of those of Fra Filippo, is oval [a]
"modelled broadly in a low and flattened relief."

Another portrait has been attributed to the Nativity o
in S. Margherita of Prato, and now in the Louvre, where
Virgin kneels in adoration before the Jesu.

But this painting, though assigned to Fra Lippo, has b
asserted by modern critics to belong in its style to a diffe[r]
class of work, to some painter belonging to the naturali[st]

The Peselli.   school of Uccello, Castagno, Baldovinetti, and the Peselli.

"It is, in fact, a work such as Francesco Peselli
Pesellino might have produced, and which was proba[bly]
painted by him under the influence of the Carmelite friar."

Giuliano   Born at Florence in 1367, Giuliano d'Arrigo, know[n]
Pesello,
from 1367.   Pesello, was a child of the 14th century. "He m[ay]
"have witnessed the death of Taddeo Gaddi, have heard
"praises of Giovanni da Milano or of Orcagna. He lived
"laboured in the Giottesque period."

Examples.   Giuliano was a sculptor and architect as well as a pai[nter].
He worked on a portion of the frieze of the tabernacl[e]
Or San Michele in 1414–16. He competed for the erectio[n]
the cupola of S. Maria de' Fiore in 1419, and in 1420 was
pointed as a sort of understudy (provveditore) to Brunelle[schi]
a post which he held for several years.

His wife, Mona Bartolomea, had borne him two daughters, and his son-in-law having died in bad circumstances, the grandson came to live with him, and grew up to be a painter of fame, known as Pesellino. "Vasari confounds the names, the relationship, the work of the two painters, and the confusion which he thus created is all but inextricable at the present day." [*Francesco di Stefano Pesel-called Pesellino, from 1422–57.*]

But Pesellino of course belonged entirely to another epoch of art; he is influenced by Uccello and del Castagno, and probably Vasari is right in saying that he imitated Fra Filippo.

In this connection may be noticed Morelli's remark, that though Masaccio's frescoes must have made a profound impression upon him, as is testified by many of his figures, his true master, as Vasari had stated, was Fra Filippo: and the same critic, who possessed two of his paintings, a "S. Jerome" and a panel of "Griselda's Marriage," now both in the Bergamo Gallery, calls attention to Pesellino's predilection for grey, blue, and violet tones, to the rounded folds of his drapery, to the similarity of his hands and ears, and even of the type of his heads, with those of Fra Lippo.

Hence several of the works which have been assigned to Fra Filippo are possibly due to Pesellino; examples are the Nativity of the Louvre just mentioned, another Nativity with figure of S. John Baptist and saints also in the Louvre, and the predella of Fra Lippo's altar-piece of S. Croce is assigned by Vasari and others to Pesellino. Perhaps, however, the masterpiece of his remaining works is the Trinità of the National Gallery, questioned, however, by Morelli, but given to him by Vasari. In his altar-piece of the Annunciation, still in the Sisterhood of S. Giorgio at Florence, he comes nearer to Alesso Baldovinetti, who was born very little later than himself. [*Examples.*] [*Alesso Baldovinetti, 1427–99.*]

But few of Baldovinetti's works remain to us, partly, perhaps, from his having essayed new mediums in fresco which were not durable. A fresco of the Nativity, in the church of [*Examples.*]

the S. Annunziata in Florence, which is in very bad conditio
an altar-piece, now in the Uffizi Gallery, and a Trinity wi
saints, painted for the Chapel of the Gianfigliazzi at S. Trini
of Florence, and now in the Florentine Academy, are amoi
the few reliable works remaining, while his portrait in fres
(from S. Trinità) came into the late Signor Morelli's collectic
Alesso worked also at mosaic on the front of S. Miniato
Monte and the Baptistery of Florence; he died on the 29
August 1499, and was buried in S. Lorenzo.

Fra Filippo—continued.

To return now to Fra Filippo, it is only fair to the fri
to state that the whole story of Lucretia Buti has be
questioned by modern critics, together with the more fantast
one of his capture by Barbary pirates, and his having be
locked in by Cosmo de Medici to finish his work, and letti
himself out of the window by sheets tied together, in quest
midnight adventures.

All this last is probably mere legend, but recent doc
mentary evidence (especially Filippino's will, leaving anni
provision for his mother Lucretia, daughter of Francesco Bu
seems to confirm the story of the seduction at Prato.

At least Fra Filippo was certainly poor, judging from l
complaints on that topic, and certainly industrious; he see
to have been burdened with relatives, and generally in debt.

Examples.

His last days were spent at Spoleto, where he adorned t
apse of the cathedral with scenes from the Life of the Virgir

"Those who have not examined those frescoes," sa
Mr. Symonds, "ruinous in their decay and spoilt by stuj
" restoration, can form no just notion of the latent capacity
" this great master. The whole of the half-dome above t
" tribune is filled with a 'Coronation of the Madonna.'
" circular rainbow surrounds both her and Christ. She
" kneeling with fiery rays around her, glorified by
" assumption into heaven. Christ is enthroned, and at l
" side stands a seat prepared for His mother, as soon as
" crown that He is placing on her head shall have made
" Queen. From the outer courts of heaven, thronged w

multitudes of celestial beings, angels are crowding in, breaking the lines of the prismatic aureole, as though the ardour of their joy could scarcely be repressed ; while the everlasting light of God sheds radiance from above, and far below lies earth, with diminished sun and moon."
Fra Filippo died at Spoleto in 1469, leaving his work to be finished by his pupil Fra Diamante. Gossip, which had been so busy with his life, credited even his death to poison from the relatives of a lady who had usurped Lucretia's place in his affections. His epitaph was written by the poet Angelo Politiano.

Fra Diamante (about 1430).

Fra Filippo left two more important pupils who were influenced by his teaching. "Whether Filippino Lippi was in truth his son by Lucretia Buti, a novice he is said to have carried off from her cloister at Prato, has been called in question by recent critics. . . . . There can, however, be no doubt that to the Frate, whether he was his father or only his teacher, Filippino owed his style," though Vasari tell that on his father's death, in 1469, Filippino, being still young, was guided by Sandro Botticelli.

Filippino Lippi, 1457-1504.

Morelli has noticed particularly the peculiar structure of Filippino's hands in which " the juncture with the metacarpus is so sharply defined that it has not the appearance of a natural growth, the fingers look as if they had been screwed into their places and are long, wooden, and nerveless." His landscape backgrounds seem to have been studied from nature and are often taken from the wooded lands of Tuscany ; they have been found to be darker in tone than Botticelli's.

His share in the frescoes of the Brancacci Chapel in the Carmine we have already noticed ; " lower in the scale of art than Masaccio, to whom he succeeds, Filippino still worthily fulfils the arduous task imposed upon him." He is in fact, at a disadvantage with Masaccio in certain respects, colour perhaps, and certainly in composition ; yet his fresco of the Apostles SS. Peter and Paul before the Proconsul, and still more that of the Boy restored to Life, part of which

Examples.

was completed by him, shows nothing incongruous with great master on whose work he follows. Vasari has noti his connection with Sandro Botticelli, who was like himse pupil of Fra Filippo, and whom we shall come to no immediately, as well as the painter Cosimo Roselli, who a contemporary with the two last artists, and whose best w is to be seen in the Churches of Florence, in S. Ambrogio, the entrance court of S. Annunziata—the first of the serie frescoes completed by del Sarto—and S. Maria Maddalena Pazzi. In the Ufizzi, also, he has a "Coronation of Virgin," and several other pictures.

Cosimo Roselli 1439-1507. Examples.

Of his four frescoes in the Sistine Chapel the b perhaps, is the "Sermon on the Mount," in which he assisted in the landscape by his pupil Piero de Cosimo; in these frescoes, as in his work in S. Ambrogio—as too Masaccio's paintings—the action is watched by numer figures, studies of contemporary portraiture, and full of dig and beauty. This feature was reproduced by other painter. the epoch, and especially will be noticed later in the work Ghirlandajo. "Simple and tranquil," says one writer, "in " costume of their time, they stand by as spectators, or rat " witnesses of the holy incident represented, and freque " occupy the principal places in the picture. They are g " rally arranged somewhat symmetrically in detailed gro " thus giving the whole a peculiarly solemn effect."

Filippino Lippi —continued.

Filippino himself seems to have had no lack of com sions; he painted in 1487 the Strozzi Chapel in Santa M Novella at Florence, and passing through Spoleto, on his to Rome, he erected a monument at the expense of Lorenz Medici "to the pictorial virtues of Fra Filippo." In R Filippino was employed by the Cardinal Oliviero Caraff paint the walls of the Caraffa Chapel of S. Maria S Minerva, and a letter from him to Filippo Strozzi fixes work here to 1489.

"The Triumph of S. Thomas Aquinas" and "Miracle of S. John" are remarkable for an almost inso display of Roman antiquities, not studied, it need scarcel served, with the scientific accuracy of an Alma-Tadema, painted with a kind of passion. "To this delight in antique details Filippino added violent gestures, strained attitudes, and affected draperies." Before Filippino's return Florence his patron Filippo Strozzi had been carried off by ith ; his next work is at Prato, and in the altar-piece of Donato al Scopeto, now in the Uffizi Gallery of Florence, rivals Fra Filippo in the pyramidal composition of an Adoration of the Magi," containing more than thirty figures. To be noticed, too, is his "Marriage of S. Catherine" t. Dominic, Bologna, dated 1501) and his "Madonna and ild, with SS. Jerome and Dominic" (note the deep colouring d the finely-drawn heads), now in the National Gallery, as ll as the exquisite "Adoring Angel" (in fresco) there also. His frescoes of Madonna with Angels and Saints, for a bernacle of Prato, is one of his most delightful works, and is ll of capriciously detailed ornament, of arabesques and masks ; t his later works, especially after the close of the century. ow failing power, which is marked, indeed, in those frescoes the Strozzi Chapel which the heirs of Filippo induced the tist at length to complete.

And here may be mentioned briefly an artist with great Rafaellino del dividual tenderness of charm, Rafaellino del Garbo, the pupil Garbo, 1466– Filippino, under whose name his works have frequently 1524. peared. We may instance among these the picture of the unich Gallery, given to Filippino by Cavalcaselle, bu: rmised by Frizzoni, and later by Morelli, to be a work by ifaellino ; here, too, should be mentioned his work of the orence Academy, "The Resurrection," with its vigour of pression, and the two excellent pictures of the Berlin llery (Madonna and Angels) which are far preferable to the uvre example.

It is with such an artist as Sandro Botticelli that one feels Sandro Filipepi th most regret the limitation of space which such an (known as alysis as this imperatively involves. "In an age when the celli), 1447– lives of artists were full of adventure, his life is almost 1515.

E

" colourless. . . . He did not even go by his true name
" Sandro is a nickname, and his true name is Filipepi
" Botticelli being only the name of the goldsmith who firs
" taught him art. Only two things happened to him, tw
" things which he shared with other artists—he was invite
" to Rome to paint in the Sistine Chapel, and he fell in late
" life under the influence of Savonarola, passing apparentl
" almost out of men's sight in a sort of religious melanchol
" which lasted till his death in 1515, according to the receive
" date."

Filippino had painted his portrait among the spectato
of the martyrdom of S. Peter in the Brancacci Chapel—"
" sullen and sensual looking man in profile, whose head
" remarkable for the salience of the nose, the deep set of th
" eye under the pent-house of the brow, the heaviness of th
" under-jaw, and the size of a large and fleshy mouth."
purple cap confines his long flowing locks, and a red mant
shrouds his form. Apprenticed at first to a goldsmith, h
interest turned to painting, and as we have seen, Fra Filip
was the artist on whom he modelled his style. "No paint
" of the 15th century illustrates better than Botticelli th
" various changes which the art of his time had undergo
" . . . . He enjoyed the fruits gathered with labour
" conscientious students of perspective; and felt the influen
" of those who combined the experience of plastic art a
" pictorial art. He personified the condition of the art of
" time, and, being of an impetuous character, embodied m
" of its defects with some of its qualities."

He was just past the age of twenty-five when Fra Filip
died, and to the years immediately succeeding may be assign
some of his circular paintings bearing the impress of the Frat
influence, probably among them the exquisite round of
Coronation of Madonna, now in the Gallery of the Uffizi.

"That masterpiece combines all Botticelli's best qualiti
" For rare distinction of beauty in the faces it is uniq
" while the mystic calm and resignation, so misplaced in
" Aphrodites, find a meaning here." The fact that he

[By Sandro Botticelli] THE CORONATION OF THE VIRGIN. [UFFIZI GALLERY, FLORENCE. (Fotog. Alinari.)

commissioned by the Signori of Florence to paint the Pazzi conspirators, who had murdered Giuliano de Medici in 1478, shows his position then to have been good ; for the Medici he painted the Adoration of the Magi, intended especially to honour the deceased Cosimo—a picture now in the Uffizi Gallery, and in which Vasari gives two of the Magi as being portraits of Giuliano and Giovanni de Medici—as well as the lately discovered "Athena and Satyr" (Pitti Palace). The period of 1481–84, about which time he was called to Rome with Ghirlandajo, Perugino, Luca Signorelli, and others, was a period of great activity with Sandro. It was perhaps at this time that he illustrated with designs an edition of Dante, and now, too, in the great Coronation of the Virgin, to be seen in the Florentine Academy, he realises the idea of infinity and space, in the motion of the glad angels who pass flowers to one another or scatter them on the floor of heaven.

To be compared with this, in its rapturous sense of divine gladness, is the Nativity of the National Gallery, painted, it is thought, in the year 1500, in which Mr. Monkhouse remarks that we see " that intensity of feeling, which is the peculiar
' characteristic of Botticelli, strained to its highest pitch. It
' does not need the inscription upon it to tell us that it was pro-
' duced under great excitement." Yet if we are entranced, as his writer, before the ecstatic dance of the angels in heaven, and their rapturous meeting with the redeemed on earth, we may yet pause to compare with it the same passionate intensity in the " Calumny of Apelles " (Uffizi), where the very statues seem to sway with the energy of its movement, and in the Miracle of S. Zenobio " of the Dresden Gallery. But in this Nativity " of the London Gallery we seem to feel the very spirit of the Piagnone, painting but two years after Savonarola's death, and still inflamed with the Vision of Christ's Kingdom come on earth, while a calmer spirit breathes in the wistful Madonna of the same collection.

At Rome, in the Sistine Chapel, Botticelli touched scenes from the Old Testament, from the wandering of the Hebrews under Moses, with his quaint grace of fluttering draperies and rich detailed ornament; in the designs for Dante, as Mr. Pater observes, "the scene of the Centaurs wins us at once, for, "forgetful of the actual circumstances of their appearance, "Botticelli has gone off with delight to the thought of the "Centaurs themselves, bright small creatures of the woodland, "with arch baby faces and mignon forms, drawing tiny bows."

We are fortunate in being able to include in our illustrations that beautiful Madonna and Child, with attending angels, which is one of the gems of the Berlin Gallery; this collection, which is so rich in the pre-Raphaelite masters, has another genuine and beautiful Botticelli, the S. Sebastian, as well as the "Venus," which is evidently a study for the same goddess at the Uffizi,—which last, however, Morelli attributes not to the master but to his school. In this attribution he is influenced by the "intensive evidence,"* for while Fra Filippo imitated in his stumpy, awkward hands his prototypes Fra Angelico and Masaccio, and adhered to the semi-round form of ear, "Botticelli's hands, on the contrary, are very bony and plebeian "and the nails broad and square, with sharp dark outlines. "These characteristic hands, together with the large nostrils, "the movement and the elongated folds of the drapery, and "the brilliant transparency of colour, in which a golden "cherry-red predominates, make Botticelli's paintings easy to "distinguish from those of his imitators." To be noticed, too, are this painter's landscape backgrounds, always idealized and showing jagged rocks, and "often winding river banks or inlets of the sea"; and a good example of his typical forms is the "Calumny of Apelles" in the Uffizi Collection.

Botticelli, indeed, lived in a generation of naturalists, and he might have been a mere naturalist among them. "There "are traces enough in his work of that alert sense of outward "things which, in the pictures of that period, fills the lawns "with delicate living creatures, and the hillsides with pools "of water, and the pools of water with flowering reeds."

---

* See Appendix III.

It is in this sympathy with things beautiful in nature—which makes him so model his roses that every curl in their frail petals is rendered "with as much care as though they were the hands or feet of Graces"—that Botticelli comes near to another contemporary Florentine painter, the pupil of Cosimo Roselli, called Piero di Cosimo. "Piero was by Piero di Cosimo, 1462-1521 "nature and employment a decorative painter, the construction "of cars for pageants, and the adornment of dwelling rooms "and marriage chests, affected his whole style, rendering it "less independent and more quaint than that of Botticelli. "Landscape occupies the main part of his composition, made "up by a strange amalgam of the most eccentric details, rocks "tumbling over blue bays, sea caverns, and fantastic mountain "ranges."

Morelli has noticed this painter's interest in landscape, which he shared with Pinturicchio, Costa and Gozzoli, and adds that his earlier works point to Filippino's influence.

His quaint humours are mentioned with delight by Vasari; but the point which connects him with Botticelli is the romantic treatment of classical mythology, which finds an example in the Perseus and Andromeda of the Uffizi Gallery, and also in that charming painting of the Murdered Procris watched by a Satyr, now in the National Gallery. Examples.

"In creating this Satyr the painter has not had recourse to any antique bas-relief, but has imagined for himself a being, half-human, half-bestial, and wholly real; nor has he portrayed a Procris a nymph of Greek form, but a girl of Florence. The strange animals and gaudy flowers introduced into the landscape background further remove the subject from the sphere of classic treatment."

Nor are these remarks less true of his delightful Mars and Venus with Cupid, of the Berlin Gallery, where there is just this same quaint note in the dainty flowered background, in the rabbits that peep out from behind the recumbent forms; while in his Warrior in Armour of the National Gallery we have a portrait full of dignity and beauty, as well as interesting

from its background of the Palazzo Publico of Florence, w
Marzocco and the Loggia de' Lanzi.

Sandro Botticelli— continued.

It is this blending of mediævalism with the classic legen
the quaint touch upon mythology only half understood, t
affects a whole group of Botticelli's work, and gives it
individuality, a fascination, that is all its own. " It was
" doubt with a kind of wonder that the artist heard of Fai
" and Sylvans, and the birth of Aphrodité from the wav
" Such fables took deep hold upon their fancy, stirring th
" to strange and delicate creations, the offspring of their o
" thought, and no mere copies of marbles seen in sta
" galleries." This quaintness of touch, this blending of t
diverse laws, appears in all Sandro's work, and gives to it
peculiar character; it springs in part no doubt from
condition of the epoch, in part, too, perhaps, from his individ
temperament.

Examples.

We find it in his exquisite Primavera—now in
Accademia of Florence—inspired by the verse of Lucreti
and one of the most poetic of his works : " and yet the t
" spirit of the Latin verse has not been seized 1
" something special to the artist and significant for Medice
" scholarship has been added." We see it sometimes becom
almost grotesque—as in the Aphrodité of the National Galle
or the Mars and Venus of the same collection—where 1
goddess, draped in thin raiment, looks out wearily, wh
dainty goat-footed Cupids play with the armour of her sleepi
lover. We find it again in all the fulness of its dreamy bea
in that Birth of Aphrodité in the Gallery of the Uffizi;
which he has thought of Love's goddess being wafted
the shore by the attendant Zephyrs, poised on a dain
lipped shell that moves over the crisping waves to where,
the bank, Flora holds out her flower embroidered man
Had he taken his theme from the poet? or had Ang
Politiano drunk in the dreamy imaginings of the painter—
he watched the naked goddess, with her subtly modelled li
and meshes of hair of pure gold, when he wrote for Giuli
de' Medici those stanzas of the " Giostra " that describe

THE BIRTH OF VENUS FROM THE WAVES
(UFFIZI GALLERY, FLORENCE.)

BY SANDRO BOTTICELLI

(See p. 70)

birth of wave-born Venus—or described in his canzone "*lo nanellato crin dall' aurea testa*" (the inwoven folds of the golden tresses) of that fairest Simonetta whom Sandro too had painted? Or had the painter who set in the eyes of Venus the same incommunicable sadness that dwells in his Madonna's face, when she looks out over the happy sleeping Child—had the artist who sought to comment Dante's poem, and was moved to strange remorse by Savonarola's thundering words—had he too sought, and sought in vain, to solve in his own character the choice of opposing messages, the Enigma that lay deep in the soul of the Renaissance—one day too surely to work out its answer?

We must close our notice of the painter thus with a note of interrogation, and turn to one who in many respects is his antithesis, and yet held as great a place in the art of his time—the painter Domenico Ghirlandajo.

Domenico Bigordi (called Domenico Ghirlandajo 1449-98.

Born in 1449, "Ghirlandajo's talent was of slow and " majestic growth. His father describes him at the age of " thirty-one as without a fixed place of abode, and he does " not seem to have enjoyed the privileges of a master till " after the completion of a series of frescoes in the Church of " Ognissanti, in one of which he depicted Amerigo Vespucci, " who was 'to give his name to a continent, and, as he sat, " ' was perhaps unconscious of his future greatness.'" Yet Domenico's progress, if slow, had been not less sure and thorough ; contemning the mere practice of altar-pieces, he sought in fresco the qualities of breadth and dignity which appealed to his strongly tempered mind, and in the observation of Giotto's masterpieces, and—yet even more—in the close and attentive study of those frescoes that Masaccio had left in the Brancacci Chapel of the Carmine, he found the qualities on which to base his style.

There was a difference of but two years in age between Ghirlandajo and Botticelli, of whom Monkhouse observes, that to judge them by their works Ghirlandajo had one of the most phlegmatic, Botticelli one of the most sanguine of temperaments.

We may compare their work in portraiture in the Nation
Gallery—the determined characterization of the young man
a red cap, which is now generally ascribed to Botticelli, wi
the "Portrait of a Youth," or still more the "Bust Portrait
a Girl," by Domenico in the same collection. "One observes a

Examples.
"remembers less of herself than of her costume. It is easi
"to forget her face than her elaborate coiffure, the ornamen
"on her dress, with its rich arrangement of reds and orang
"and yellows, or even the beautiful jewels on the shelf besi
"her. As she appears here, she appears in Ghirlandajo's fres
"of the 'Salutation of the Virgin,' in S. Maria Novella, one
"the attendants or friends of S. Elizabeth, with the same lon
"stiff neck and round bust, standing at the entrance of
"magnificent palace, with the same air—calm, dignified, a
"indifferent."

From his teacher, Baldovinetti, Domenico perhaps gain
that interest in mosaic which made him, in comparing painti
with the work of the mosaicist exclaim, "that the first w
fleeting, the last eternal." Yet more still did he gath
in the harvest reaped by each worker in anatomy, chiaroscu
and perspective—by such men as Uccello, the Peselli, or the
masters in plastic art, the Pollajuoli—and resume, we may se
in his art those qualities of science and sound technique whi
led up to the greatness of "that marvellous Florentine schoo

The frescoes to which I have alluded in the Vespu
Chapel of the Ognissanti at Florence have unfortunate
been destroyed, but those in the body of the church and
the refectory remain—including a S. Jerome which may
compared with his noble kneeling figure of that saint in t
Berlin Museum—both bearing the date of 1480; in t
refectory Ghirlandajo has painted the Last Supper with
dignity of attitude which suggests the later work of Leonar
but neither here nor in his later purely decorative frescoes
the Sala del Orologio in the Palazzo Vecchio (1481–85)
the qualities of his complete style yet fully apparent.

Many of the artists employed on the Palazzo Pubblico, among whom were Botticelli, Perugino, Filippino Lippi and others, were summoned to Rome by Sixtus IV. to decorate at time the Sixtine Chapel, and Ghirlandajo was among those who obeyed the Papal summons.

On his way he would seem to have painted the fresco of the Annunciation in the Oratory of S. Giovanni at Gimignano, while at Rome (1475) he produced a work worthy of his completed genius, and in which he has been said to surpass all his contemporaries, in his fresco of the calling of S. Peter and S. Andrew in the Capella Sistina, in which his early study of Masaccio's style bears its full fruit.

Stopping at S. Gimignano again, perhaps on his return, more probably later, in 1487, he painted the frescoes of the Capella S. Fina, representing the death of that saint, which is one of his most masterly creations.

Equally powerful in choice of form, in perspective, and unity of design, are those frescoes which he has painted subsequently, perhaps, to his Cenacolo in the Convent of Marco—in the family chapel of the Sassetti in S. Trinità at Florence. Here, again, he introduces that mingling of classical and sacred subjects which perhaps gave Perugino a suggestion for his work in the Sala del Cambio, while in his sketch of S. Francis in this series, he perhaps loses in contrast with Giotto's treatment of this theme in imagination and simplicity of rendering; but makes up by a dignified and noble realism, by the accuracy of modelling, and the perfection of his technique. Indeed Ghirlandajo had not, even at his best, the qualities which make up a great imaginative painter; he deserves the place of honour "not because he had the keenest intuitions, the deepest thoughts, the strongest passion, the subtlest fancy, the loftiest imagination—for in all these points he was excelled by some one or other of his contemporaries or predecessors—but because his intellect was the most comprehensive, and his mastery of art the most complete."

There is something irritating," says Mr. Symonds, " in pure common sense imported into art, and Ghirlandajo's

" masterpieces are the apotheosis of that quality. How co
" how judicious, how sagacious, how mathematically ord
" we exclaim ; but we gaze without emotion, and we
" away without regret. . . . . It is a positive reli
" think that Ghirlandajo sighed in vain to have the circu
" the walls of Florence given him to paint. How he v
" have covered them with compositions, stately, flowing,
" sober, and incapable of stirring any feeling in the soul.'

Hardly had Domenico finished his fresco in S. T
than he was requested to renew the choir of S. Maria No
and replace the damaged masterpieces of Andrea Orcagna

The Ricci, who were patrons of the altar, had been
by Giovanni Tornabuoni to permit the decoration t
completed by Ghirlandajo at his own patron's expense
in the lowest fresco, the artist has painted the portra
Giovanni Tornabuoni and his wife ; the whole chape
divided into four courses of frescoes on the three
among which the " Birth of the Virgin " is perhaps th
which is most justly celebrated.

In this fresco the careful perspective of the archite
and the use of rich classic ornament is most apparent
figure of the girl pouring water shows the artist's lo
imitating drapery in its movement, while elsewhere
precise outline of forms and features seems to vie with p
work in gold or bronze. "The chapel was opened
" completion in December, 1490 ; but the window, with d
" of Ghirlandajo . . . . was not finished till 1491.
" may picture the jubilant crowd of Tornabuoni and Tornaq
" Sassetti, Medici, all of whom had sat in turn to Dom
" for their portraits, present at the opening. We may
" the congratulations heaped upon Ghirlandajo,. the e
" sion of his fame, and the commissions which overwh
" him.

" Domenico was to receive 12 hundred ducats for certai
" two hundred more, contigent on the painter's succe
" pleasing his patron. Giovanni Tornabuoni admitted t
" was pleased, but begged Ghirlandajo not to press f

contingent sum; and the artist nobly declared himself satisfied, showing, in the ordinary business of life, the calm and repose which seemed to dictate his every action and touched its influence on his painting." Illustration of this ose of temperament is the quaint story which tells how Vallombrosa the hard cakes and watery soup placed before m by the Abbot were accepted tranquilly by Domenico, roused the ire of his brother David, who broke the soup een over the prior's head, and told his Superior that his ther's fame was greater than that of all the beggarly bots of the monastery.

Domenico was assisted in his work by this brother David, o was with him when painting in the Sistina, and by ther brother, Benedetto, who has left us an indifferent work he Louvre (Christ going to Calvary). His brother-in-law stiano Mainardi (died 1513) is an artist of more importance, l to be distinguished by his delicacy of characterization, may be observed in his figures of saints. His works are be found in the churches of his birth-place, S. Gimignano; Crowe remarks of Ghirlandajo's fresco of the Annunciation" in the Pieve of S. Gimignano, "The style of this piece betrays already the help of Sebastian Mainardi, Ghirlandajo's brother-in-law and assistant, especially in the igure of Gabriel." Other works from his hand are in Louvre Gallery (Virgin and Child), S. Croce of Florence, especially in the Chapel of S. Fina at S. Gimignano, where worked with Domenico in 1487. Ghirlandajo's pupil ncesco Granacci (1477-1543), who came later under hael Angelo's influence, and his son Ridolfo, who inclined Leonardo, will perhaps be better treated of in the succeeding iod.

Typical too, though in a less pleasing way, of Domenico's racter is the report that he told his assistants "to refuse to commission that should be brought to his shop, were it even for ladies' petticoat paniers, and that if they did not choose to accept them he would"; typical perhaps, in its occupation with finite aims, of the prosaic, the unemotional

qualities of his style and personal genius. "He
" Ghirlandajo did but reflect the temper of his age, t
" temper which Cosimo de Medici, the greatest patron botl
" art and scholarship, in Florence before 1470, represen
" in his life and public policy." While in the great quali
of his art, in its sanity, its careful science, its plastic note,
love of portraiture, of classic ornament and detail, Dome
sums up the qualities of the Florentine craftsmen who prece
him, and points the path to the approaching masters of the
Renaissance.

Here, then, we have reached a point in our analysis wh
we may pause, where we may glance back for a moment v
benefit over the ground we have now traversed. And {
ground, it will be observed, has been mainly covered by
art of Florence; if Pisa, if Siena have sometimes interver
and given, in the one case, an impulse to sculpture, in
other a softer sense of beauty, a more emotional renderin;
mediæval faith, yet it is Florence in her keen, clear intell
in her precision, as of dainty goldsmith's work, in the sa
and the science of her art, who gives to all Italy, to all
world indeed, the keynote of the future, who makes it poss
for the art of the Revival, as we know and prize it, to h
existed at all.

Giotto is the innovator, the typical Florentine, industric
religious withal, but by no means mystical, by no me
devoted to the cowl and the cloister; Ghirlandajo is
conclusion, the man who typically sums for us those g
Florentine qualities—almost too sane, too clear-headed,
unemotional. And between these two what an array, wh
diversity of talent, what numbers of faces—clear cut, earn
intellectual, with their long hair pressed under the burgh
scarlet cap, just as we see them in Masaccio's or Cosir
frescoes—press in upon us, and claim their part in the g
movement that they loved and lived in. The age
mediævalism is already past, the age when the artist exi
only to give bodily concrete form to the legends, the dogr
the doctrines which the Church would impress upon

ul ; the age of the Revival has begun, the age when men
d back to the world as with newly opened eyes ; when
dreamed that for them too there was almost a Paradise on
, in this rich, living world around them, in the clouds and
lue sky, the flowers, the stretch of distant meadows, with
d them the blue Apennines, and that white wonder, the
ellous beauty of curve and complex line, in the forms of
; men and women.

,d there came then the reaction, the inevitable swing of
)endulum, that was expressed in Angelico's paintings,
vanarola's tremendous sermons. Was it for nothing then
he Church, sealed with the blood of Saints and Martyrs,
,ointed the way to God ? That true path to Heaven, was
the annihilation of this tumultuous self, the consecration
ery thought and passion and feeling to the mystic and
life ? Was not the Soul the one thing, greater than all
eauty of this living world, of this sin-stained, earthly
? Before these very men, who look at us from these old
)es with their tense clear-cut lips, with their eager,
)nate eyes, the Enigma lay waiting, Sphinx-like in its
and its intensity.

r was not this true above all, this message that God's
;h had brought down through the ages, that pealed out
every church and every cloister in His Christendom ?
yet how abandon this Self, this Personality, so intense
it epoch, so individual, so all absorbing ! How could they
this world of beauty so newly recovered, so marvellous,
xhaustible in its power of knowledge and delight ? For
ly they lived, not alone in the present, and yet far less in
ıst ages of cloistered faith ; from out of the dead world of
ıendom and Empire dim forms seemed to arise, more
ʏ and more exquisite than man, it seemed, had ever
ıed—forms of dead gods and goddesses waking before
very eyes to life—Aphrodité and Hera and golden-
red Phœbus, Pan with the riotous Fauns and the-
-limbed Nymphs that haunt the woods and waves.

It was like opium to them, this breath out of ᵢ
beautiful dead past, that crept up and encircled them in
magic ; no preaching could reach them then, no priest or mc
really bring them back into the old narrow ways that h
sufficed their forefathers.

We watch them, like men spellbound, ceasing to cɪ
greatly for war or politics or almost futurity, expressing w
their whole souls this marvellous dream that was hold
them, in forms of hybrid and strangely fascinating beau
grasping with their whole powers of life at yet fartl
completer, more satisfying expression and knowledge.

They sit as in a dream, these men of the Reviv
absorbed, enslaved, unconscious, while behind them, in sɪ
vision as one wiser Italian saw, we too might see the toss
of horses' heads, the glint of spears, and the earth trembl
beneath the tramp of armies—all the half-savage feudal hc
of France and Spain and Germany on their way already o
sea and mountains to pour their savagery, their brutal lust ᵢ
fury, into that lovely land of art and beauty, to ravage ᵢ
torture and kill and burn, till they have crushed and ensla
that fairest Italy, till they have stamped out in blood and
the golden hope of her Revival.

It is a strange picture—perhaps one of the strangest ᵢ
most terrible of the world's history ; it is before this pict
that we must leave the reader, as we end the first part of
analysis of the art of the Italian Revival.

APPENDICES.

APPENDIX I.

Painting in Tempera and Fresco.

To understand the work of the early Italian painters it will be of help to know something of their methods of work, which affected very largely the qualities of the work itself. These may be divided practically into two—painting in tempera, and painting in fresco ; the use of oil colours came in, of course, a good deal later.

In a general way, as Sir C. Eastlake has pointed out, the word tempera was used in the sense of "mixture" (*cf.* Pliny, "temperare unguentum"), so that in the wider application tempera meant for an Italian "any more or less fluid medium with which pigments "may be used," and Vasari says of oil painting, "L'olio e la tempera loro." But in a more specialized sense, tempera means painting with a glutinous (and not an oily) medium, as, for instance, egg, size, or gum, or any binding substance soluble in water, and, more specifically still, it means a medium in which yolk of egg is the main ingredient, the milky juice of the fig being sometimes added.

In these remarks I have been guided by the judgment of that most lucid art writer, the late Mr. Hamerton. He says : "Water " is not, strictly speaking, the medium of tempera painting, but it " is the diluent of the medium, and consequently tempera may " be not unfairly regarded as a sort of water-colour painting. . " . . Tempera is, in fact, body colour with an egg medium, " and a watery diluent." The qualities of tempera painting, as practised by the Italians, are generally great brilliancy of colour, combined with delicacy and precision of line, qualities which are attractive in themselves and most decorative, even when they connote a want of our present knowledge of aerial perspective. Though subsequent varnishing is often deceptive, creating an erroneous impression of oil painting, yet these qualities may be studied without difficulty in the work of the early and many of the later Italians (*e.g.*, Crivelli), and perhaps no better example of them can be selected than that portrait of Isotta di Rimini which Mr. Hamerton has chosen for illustration, painted by Piero della Francesca, and now in the London National Gallery.

She is not exactly the beauty whom we should have expected to have enslaved the critical Pandolfo's wandering affections (*see* Leo Batt. Alberti, p. 32), but we shall notice the delicacy and beauty of the profile, and though the dress has faded, the rich jewellery shows love of detail, and clearness of colour.

Tempera was killed by oil painting, the new medium that possessed such richness of effect and obvious advantages, which in another note we may come to speak of.

Let us now turn to Fresco, an essentially different process, which has been defined as "the art of painting on fresh plaster, " which dries with the colours and fixes them." This freshness of the plaster is, therefore, an essential condition of fresco, and for this purpose over the first rough coat on the wall (of river sand and lime, generally on brickwork) a second coat, called by the Italian craftsmen the "intonaco," is laid, of fine sand and well prepared lime, and on this the artist has to work.

He can only work while it is wet, because the drying of the plaster must fix his colours ; and, therefore, the plasterer accompanies him, and lays on the amount of "intonaco" required for that day's work, removing it if an error has been made.

If the latter event occurs often it becomes an exasperating process, both for artist and plasterer ; and in the experiments made this century in England for the decoration of the Houses of Parliament it seems to have literally driven two of the plasterers mad, one melancholy and the other raving.

These experiments were not considered very satisfactory, but the spirit fresco, a modern development which it lies out of my province here to describe, was used with success by Lord Leighton in his frescoes of South Kensington ("Arts of War and Peace "), and he has himself called it a delightful medium, easy to manipulate, and in its results highly satisfactory. Fresco was no doubt popular in Italy because it was suited for architectural decoration, was rapid, fairly durable and cheap, and induced by its conditions a broad and simple method of treatment.

No doubt this latter is the reason why Michael Angelo spoke of it in such commendation, and why the best artists from Giotto to Buonarrotti put their best work into this medium.

This is why, too, Italian art can never be really grasped in its entirety without a visit to Italy, since the panel paintings and altar-pieces of collections never called out the soul of the artist as did this immediate, intense, broad grasp required in fresco. It will be easy to multiply examples of this truth, which I do not think that I have at all overstated. Giotto Bondone in the vast mural decorations of the Arena Chapel at Padua, and S. Francesco at Assissi, Fra Lippo at Prato and Spoleto, Mantegna in the Eremitani Chapel, Spinello and Gozzoli, and the unknown creator of the "Triumph of Death," in the Pisan Campo Santo, the Lorenzetti in the Town Hall and Pinturricchio in the Libreria of Siena, Masaccio in the Brancacci Chapel, Rafaelle in the Stanze of the Vatican and Michael Angelo in the Sistina, all show us the best of themselves within the necessarily limited conditions implied by this fascinating art of Fresco.

APPENDIX II.

TACTILE VALUES.

In his theory of what he calls "tactile values," or "values of touch," Mr. Berensen makes a contribution to the science of art criticism which it may be of use to the student to consider.

In his little work on the "Florentine painters," which may be correctly summarized as a resumé of the work of some of the leading Florentines, mainly from the point of view of this theory, he has stated his theory in some detail.

"Psychology," he there remarks, "has ascertained that sight " alone gives us no accurate sense of the third dimension. In " our infancy, long before we are conscious of the process, the " sense of touch, helped on by muscular sensation of movement, " teaches us to appreciate depth, the third dimension both in " objects and space . . . Now painting is an art which aims " at giving an abiding impression of artistic reality with only two " dimensions. The painter must, therefore, do consciously what " we all do unconsciously, construct the third dimension. And " he can accomplish his task, only as we accomplish ours, by " giving tactile values to retinal impressions."

This may suffice at present for the theory, which amounts after all to saying that it is the business of the artist to make a living reality, containing the impression of solidity and depth, of his work, a fact which the reader of these pages will already have observed that the Florentine craftsmen had ever before them both in theory and practice, and which, too, the constant practice of the plastic arts helped them, without doubt, to realize. Let us observe now how the author exemplifies this theory among the artists he has chosen to mention. Among these, he selects three as giving special emphasis to the "tactile values"—Giotto, Fra Angelico, and Masaccio—and yet another later, Michael Angelo. Of the importance of Giotto, from this point of view, there can be no misconception. This was his special glory, as we have seen, that he gave life and reality to painting, which before had been immobile and symbolic. And however splendid we have found his sense of dramatisation, it would have been valueless had he not given the glow of life to the figures who tell his tales of love and sorrow.

But in Angelico Mr. Berensen hits on a less happy illustration of this view ; and it might be suggested that it is precisely in passing over almost entirely these second, and even third-rate painters, whose work we have found so interesting and so invaluable in the evolution of the Florentine school, that he lays himself open to this mistake. For our reader will have seen that this painter of heavenly things was unconcerned with the realism which was in full progress around him, with the intense Florentine interest in plastic art; that it is rather the divine significance, the subjective mood of consciousness produced by his work, than the objective reality, that is of value.

In Masaccio's work, of course, his statement is entirely correct, for here we have seen an artist, as original as Giotto, carrying the artistic evolution of the lesser craftsmen to a higher plane of realism, giving it atmosphere, solidity, the breath of life. And here we can sympathise thoroughly with Mr. Berensen when he exclaims (p. 29), "In later painting we shall easily find greater
" science, greater craft, and greater perfection of detail, but greater
" reality, greater significance, I venture to say, never. Dust-bitten
" and ruined though his Brancacci Chapel frescoes now are, I
" never see them without the strongest stimulation of my tactile
" consciousness. I feel that I could touch every figure, that it
" would yield a definite resistance to my touch, that I should have
" to expend thus much effort to displace it, that I could walk
" around it."

Lastly, the great Michael Angelo; and here this author has worked out his theory with very considerable interest and originality. "Now, while it remains true that tactile values can
" as Giotto and Masaccio have for ever established, be admirably
" rendered on the draped figure, yet drapery is a hindrace, and, at
" the best, only a way out of a difficulty, for we feel it masking
" the really significant, which is *the form underneath.* . . The
" artist, even when compelled to paint draped figures, will force
" the drapery to render the nude, in other words, the material
" significance of the human body. But how much more con-
" vincingly will the character manifest itself, when between its
" perfect rendering and the artist nothing intervenes. And this per-
" fect rendering is to be accomplished with the nude only." Hence, therefore, he argues, " To realize the play of muscle everywhere,
" to get the full sense of the various pressures and resistances, to
" receive the direct inspiration of the energy expended, we must
" have the nude ; for here alone can we watch those tautnesses
" of muscle, and those stretchings and relaxings and ripplings of
" skin, which, translated into similar strains on our own persons,
" make us fully realise movement." And hence, too, he adds with general accuracy of statement (yet we might put in a claim for Signorelli and some very noble craftsmen in sculpture), " The
" first person, since the great days of Greek sculpture, to com-
" prehend fully the identity of the nude with great figure art
" was Michael Angelo. Before him, it had been studied for
" scientific purposes, as an aid to rendering the draped figure. He

" saw that it was an end in itself, and the final purpose of his art.
" For him the nude and art were synonymous."

Here we must leave this theory at its most interesting point, but where the author himself has left it ; for his little work on the Venetians deals less with what he has named as "tactile values " and " movement," and more with the connection of the Venetians with the great movement of the Renaissance. This, in itself, explains very usefully the true position of his theory of " tactile values " as one factor, and one only of many, in the evolution of art, one which, in an intellectual school like the Florentine, has much importance, but might easily be overstated ; its relation to sculpture I pass by, as does the author, for it seems difficult in this case to see any possible application. Those readers who would follow out the theory in greater detail will find it best stated in the work above-mentioned, and more particularly in the " Analysis of enjoyment of painting," (p. 10), in which the author argues that form in painting "lends a higher
" co-efficient of reality to the object represented, with the
" consequent enjoyment of accelerated psychical processes, and
" the exhilarating sense of increased capacity in the observer."

APPENDIX III.

INTENSIVE CRITICISM.

A good method of approaching the subject of this note will be by asking ourselves, what have been and are the points of guidance in determining the genuine work of an Italian master.

I think there are three points which will occur to the mind of the reader, and these will be : (1) the general character of the school, and (2) of the master himself ; and what I may call (3) the documentary evidence of title.

We have now to consider that the interest in and change effected by Morelli's method is not that he denied the value of these three points of guidance, which had led so many art inquirers before him, but that he supplemented them by a closer, a more analytic study, by what I may describe as a more "intensive" criticism. In the character which expresses himself in his "Critical Studies of Italian Painters," he maintains, as his friend Sir A. H. Layard remarks, "That to form an opinion upon the
" authenticity of a picture, to judge of its merits, and to determine
" first the school of painting to which it belongs, and then by
" whom painted, it is not merely necessary to collect a number of
" facts concerning the life of the presumed author, to discover
" the exact dates of his birth and death, and to point out the
" misstatements of Vasari and other writers with respect to him.
" His identification and the genuineness of the work attributed
" to him should depend upon scientific analysis, upon an accurate
" knowledge, derived from long and careful study of his manner
" and style, and especially of his delineation of the different parts
" of the human body—or what Morelli denominates 'his treatment
" of form'—and of his peculiar sense of colour." Or, to quote Morelli's own words : "A closer study of form and technique
" soon convinced me, to my great satisfaction, that this is the
" only road which in most cases leads to the goal. As a matter of
" fact, all art historians, from Vasari down to our own day, have
" only made use of two tests to aid them in deciding the authorship
" of a work of art, intuition, or the so-called general impression,
" and documentary evidence." And he continues, " To arrive at
" a conclusion (often by no means an easy matter) the general
" impression is not sufficient. . . . Only by gaining a thorough
" knowledge of the characterization of each painter—of his forms
" and of his colouring—shall we ever succeed in distinguishing
" the genuine works of the great masters from those of their pupils

"and imitators, or even from copies; and though the method
"may not always lead to absolute conviction, it at least brings us
"to the threshold." This whole theory of the value of form in
criticism must be taken very closely with his remark immediately
following, that "every great artist sees and represents these forms
"in his own characteristic manner; hence for him they become
"characteristic, for they are by no means the result of accident
"or caprice, but of internal conditions." Hence followed the
importance which Morelli attached to the study of these forms of
the body, especially of the hand and of the ear (*e.g.*, the round
form of ear of Titian's middle period—1540-50—the long,
nervous hand, and short nose with wide nostrils, of Botticelli, or
again, the peculiarly strong base of thumb in Titian's hands of
men, *et similia*), and the student will find it extraordinary how
strong a similarity a careful study of one or another painter will
show in these particulars.

As an instance, I might mention that in a recent visit to the
Dresden Gallery I made a careful and detailed study of the hands
in Palma Vecchio's paintings in that collection, and found in all
the same rather fleshy and broad hands, with tapering fingers,
reappear with absolute iteration. Or again, to take another point,
in studying the paintings of Benvenuto Tisi (known as Garofalo),
in the same gallery, one finds his peculiar flesh tints—the dead
white of his women's flesh, the red-coloured tones of his male
figures—reappear in all his paintings. And yet again, to take an
instance from the same painter, the type of his women's heads,
the sweet oval face, set in its golden or light brown hair, appears
through all his paintings, whether it be Venus or Madonna that
she names herself, whether it be in Dresden or in the National
Gallery of London.

Here there are two points in this closer intensive criticism
which the student may add to his study of forms, namely, the
study of the type chosen, more especially in the case of idealised
female heads, and of the flesh colouring.

In both of these the creator's individuality forces its way most
strongly through the medium of his art; in the latter quite as
much as the former, since the colour sense is peculiarly a matter
of individual emotion, and in flesh colouring, which is really
radiated light reflected from the skin, no two colourists seem to
ever feel quite alike.

To these three points, all of the first importance, I will add
another, of value especially for Italian art, the nature of the
landscape backgrounds; to this, Morelli himself attached great
importance, and he has used it very effectively in his vindication
for Pinturricchio of the Vatican frescoes, which he attributes to
that artist.

To sum up very briefly. To the earlier method of criticism,
based on the general character of the school and artist, and the

documentary and contemporary evidence (in which Vasari had generally a considerable share), has been added a far closer, a more intensive method, which does not supersede the older criticism, save where its results are absolutely divergent, but which has been well compared to the revolution caused by the Darwinian system in scientific inquiry.

The points I have especially brought forward, the characteristic forms of the individual artist, together with his chosen idealised type (to be traced out by the student not only in his paintings, but also in his studies and sketches), his individuality in general, as well as more especially in flesh colouring and in his landscape backgrounds, must now be weighed by all serious inquirers into Italian art.

There may be other points brought forward which may also aid that analysis, but these, at least, must always remain of essential interest and importance.

APPENDIX IV.

THE EVOLUTION OF THE SUBJECT IN ITALIAN ART.

In a series of illustrated articles which he published some three years ago in the "Pall Mall Magazine," Mr. Grant Allen made a very interesting contribution to the study of Italian art, from a novel point of view, and one for which his own work in science thoroughly qualified him. His aim he has himself described in words which I cannot improve on. "The point of view is not,
" indeed, of the sort familiar to artists, yet even the artist will,
" perhaps, admit that it is calculated to make the outside
" observer look closer at works of art, and so to lead him on to
" higher appreciation of their technical and æsthetic aspects.
" Moreover, it suggests a method of comparison. I have tried
" to make my readers feel that no one work can be fairly or
" adequately judged by itself alone, nor even as a specimen of a
" particular school and a particular master. It must also be
" regarded as one of a long progressive series—an 'Annunciation,'
" a 'Pietà,' a 'Marriage of S. Catherine,' a 'Martyrdom of S.
" Sebastian,' a 'Resurrection,' an 'Assumption,' as the case may
" be—and it must be duly considered with reference to all the
" other pictures on the same theme that preceded or succeeded it.
" Even as a work of art it can never be completely understood in
" isolation. It falls into rank as one of a great family, a moment
" in a long line of historical development, and as such we must
" regard it, throwing ourselves back into the mental attitude of
" the men of its time, if we wish to judge rightly of its æsthetic,
" its evolutionary, and its doctrinal importance."

In other words the picture before us must be considered from the point of view of the evolution of its subject ; and considered in this light, it is wonderful to find what an identity is preserved, an identity with a difference as the individual or the "Time-Spirit" leaves his mark, yet an identity throughout of conception, of grouping, of background, even of individual figures. One might select a "Sposalizio," an "Annunciation," a "Nativity," a "Presentation in the Temple," an "Adoration of the Magi," or any among the well-trodden cycle of sacred subjects among which Mr. Grant Allen has chosen some half a dozen, for illustration ; perhaps, the Pietà, which he takes last, is the most interesting, because the identity, though existing, is less immediately obvious.

In treating of Giotto Bondone we have had to notice how the types which he, the great innovator, created often lasted for generations; and here, as elsewhere, it is the work of Giotto—in this case, in his frescoes of the Madonna dell' Arena at Padua—which gives the initial note of treatment. Of this picture Mr. Grant Allen observes: "As a whole, this is the finest flower of " Giotto's pictorial achievement. He never before or after painted " anything so consummate." And we can understand his enthusiasm when we study the tenderness of the kneeling Maries, of the weeping Magdalen who holds the dead Saviour's feet, the passion of the S. John who bends forward with outstretched arms, the direct earnestness with which the whole scene has been grasped hold of, and pictorially conveyed. And next, the author has traced out this special subject through the cloistered art of Angelico (Belle Arti, Florence), the hard sternness of the Ferrarese Cosimo Tura (Louvre), the tenderness of Francia and the science of Michael Angelo (National Gallery), up to the empty mannerism, the false histrionic sentiment of the "last vapid stage in the decline of Tuscan art," in the "Cristo Morto" of Angelo Bronzino (Uffizi Gallery, Florence).

In conclusion we may recommend this special view of Italian painting to the student's own interest and study; and since our space involves a necessarily limited treatment, we may refer him to Mr. Grant Allen's own words: "To sum up briefly, then, I " would say in one paragraph that, from the standpoint of the " evolutionist, we should regard any given early Italian work, not " primarily as a Raffael, a Giotto, or an Orcagna, but primarily as " a 'Paradiso,' a 'Nativity,' a 'S. Francis receiving the Stignata,' " a 'Doge presented by S. Mark to the Madonna.'"

We should mentally restore it to its proper order in the historical or evolutionary series, and should proceed to observe what traits it borrows from earlier treatments, what elements it foreshadows in later pictures. Then we should look at it as a specimen of its own genus as specially developed by such and such a school, and as conditioned by the general advance of art at such and such a period. . . If any man objects that such a method is not study of art, I can only answer, " Perhaps not, but it is study of evolution."

PART I.

COMPLETE INDEX

OF

ARTISTS MENTIONED.

	Page
Agostino di Duccio	35
Agostino di Giovanni	28
Agnolo di Ventura	28
Alberti (Leo Battista)	32, 81
Amadeo (Antonio)	38
Ambrogino da Milano	38
Andrea (Pisano)	6, 12, 19, 22
Andrea del Sarto, *see* Sarto.	
Angelico, Fra	26, 45, 48, 53–55, 57, 58, 68, 77, 83, 84, 90
Antonio Averulino, *see* Filarete.	
Antonio Veneziano	26
Aretino (Spinello), *see* Spinello.	
Arnolfo	7
Arrigo, Giuliano, *see* Pesello.	
Baldovinetti, Alesso	43, 60, 61, 72
Bartolo (Domenico di), *see* Domenico.	
Bartolo (Taddeo di), *see* Taddeo.	
Benedetto Bigordi, *see* Bigordi.	
Benozzo Gozzoli, *see* Gozzoli.	
Bernardo di Daddo	21, 23
Bernardus (de Florentiâ), *see* Nardo.	
Bicci (Lorenzo di)	21
Bicci di Lorenzo	21
Bicci (Nero di)	21
Bigordi, Benedetto	75
Bigordi, David	75
Bigordi (Domenico), *see* Ghirlandajo.	
Bondone, *see* Giotto (Bondone).	
Borgognone, Ambrogio	38
Botticelli, Sandro	43, 52, 63, 64, 65–71, 72, 87
Bronzino, Angelo	90
Brunelleschi, Filippo	27, 29 33, 60
Buffalmaco	11

	Page
Buonarroti (Mich.), *see* Michelangelo.	
Buoninsegna (Duccio di), *see* Duccio.	
Capanna, *see* Puccio.	
Casentino, Jacopo da	21
Castagno, Andrea del	45–46, 49, 61
Cellini, Benvenuto	44
Cenni, Giovanni	2, 3, 6, 13
Cimabue, *see* Cenni (Giov.).	
Cione (Andrea Orcagnuolo di), *see* Orcagna.	
Cione (Nardo)	21
Ciuffagni	38
Civitali, Matteo	35, 36
Cosimo (Piero di), *see* Piero.	
Cosimo Roselli, *see* Roselli.	
Costa, Lorenzo	69
Credi, Lorenzo da	46, 47
Crivelli, Carlo	81
Daddo (Bernardo di), *see* Bernardo.	
David Bigordi, *see* Bigordi.	
Delli, Dello	43
Desiderio da Settignano	37, 60
Diamante, Fra	63
Domenico di Bartolo	17
Domenico Ghirlandajo, *see* Ghirlandajo.	
Domenico Veneziano	21, 48
Don Lorenzo Monaco, *see* Lorenzo Monaco.	
Donatello	26, 30–33, 44, 46, 47, 51, 60
Donato di Niccolo di Betti Bardi, *see* Donatello.	
Doni (Paolo), *see* Uccello.	
Duccio (Agostino di), *see* Agostino.	
Duccio di Buoninsegna	13
Fabriano (Gentile da), *see* Gentile.	
Filarete, Antonio	32
Filipepi (Sandro), *see* Botticelli.	
Filippino Lippi	43, 51, 60, 62, 63–65, 66, 73
Filippo, Fra, *see* Lippi.	
Fonte (Giacomo della), *see* Quercia.	
Fra Angelico, *see* Angelico.	
Fra Diamante, *see* Diamante.	
Fra Guglielmo, *see* Guglielmo.	
Fra Lippo, *see* Lippi.	
Francesca (Piero della), *see* Piero.	
Francia	90
Fusina	38
Gaddi, Taddeo	18–19, 21, 60
Gaddi, the	53
Gano, Maestro	28
Garbo (Rafaellino del), *see* Rafaellino.	
Garofalo (Benvenuto Tisi)	87
Gentile da Fabriano	53, 56
Gerini (Niccolo di Pietro), *see* Niccolo.	
Ghiberti, Lorenzo	26–30, 41, 43

	Page
Ghirlandajo, Domenico	22, 43, 47, 50, 52, 67, 71–76
Giottino	20, 21
Giotto Bondone	3–6, 13, 18, 21, 40, 50, 52, 71, 73, 76, 82, 83, 84–90
Giunto da Pisa	2
Giovanni, Fra, see Angelico.	
Giovanni da Milano	60
Giovanni Pisano	7, 10–12, 28
Gozzoli, Benozzo	11, 43, 55–56, 57, 69, 82
Granacci, Francesco	75
Guglielmo, Fra	9
Guido, called il Modanino	38
Guido de Senis	12
Jacobus, The Monk	2
Joannes Petri de Mugello of Vicchio, see Angelico.	
Lapo	7
Leighton, Lord	82
Leonardo da Vinci	46, 47, 72, 75
Lippi (Filippino), see Filippino.	
Lippi, Fra Filippo	41, 43, 48, 57–63, 64, 65, 66, 68, 82
Lombardi, the	38
Lorenzetti, Ambrogio	14
Lorenzetti, Pietro	14
Lorenzetti, the	11, 21, 22, 23, 24, 82
Lorenzo da Credi, see Credi.	
Lorenzo Monaco, Don	53
Lorenzo di Pietro	17
Mainardi, Bastiano	43, 75
Maitani, Lorenzo	28
Majano (Benedetto da)	37
Majano (Giuliano da)	37
Mantegna, Andrea	52, 59, 82
Margheritone d'Arezzo	2, 16
Martini (Simone), see Memmi (S.).	
Masolino da Panicale	26, 43, 50, 51
Masaccio	26, 41, 43, 50–52, 63, 68, 71, 73, 76, 82, 83, 84
Matteo da Siena	17
Memmi, Lippo	16
Memmi, Simone	14–16
Michelangelo Buonarroti	29, 39, 75, 82, 83, 84, 85, 90
Michelozzo Michelozzi	31–32, 54
Mino da Fiesole	35–36, 38
Modanino, il, see Guido (called il Modanino).	
Montano d'Arezzo	16
Nardo Cione, see Cione (Nardo).	
Niccola Pisano	6–9, 12, 21
Niccolo di Pietro Gerini	16
Nicholas Bartolommeus of Foggia	8
Nino Pisano	20
Orcagna, Andrea	12, 21–25, 54, 60, 74, 90
Palma Vecchio	87
Panicale (Masolino da), see Masolino.	
Parri Spinelli	16
Perugino (Pietro)	67, 73

	Page
Peselli, the	50, 60, 72
Pesellino, Francesco	43, 58, 61
Pesello (Giuliano Arrigo, called Pesello)	60
Piero di Cosimo	69-70
Piero della Francesca	48-50, 81
Pinturicchio	69, 82, 87
Pisano (Andrea), *see* Andrea P.	
Pisano (Giovanni), *see* Giovanni P.	
Pisano (Niccola), *see* Niccola P.	
Pisano (Nino), *see* Nino.	
Pollajuoli, the	41, 44, 45, 47, 50, 72
Pollajuolo, Antonio	44-45
Pollajuolo, Jacopo	44
Pollajuolo, Piero	44-45, 47
Pontedera (Andrea), *see* Andrea.	
Puccio Capanna	20, 21
Quercia (Giacomo della)	28-29, 37
Rafaelle Santi, of Urbino	51, 82, 90
Rafaellino del Garbo	65
Ridolfo Ghirlandajo	75
Robbia (the della)	26
Robbia, Andrea della	34
Robbia, Luca della	34
Rosselli, Cosimo	43, 64, 76
Rossellino, Antonio	35, 36
Rossellino, Bernardo	36
Santi (Rafaelle), *see* Rafaelle.	
Sarto, Andrea del	64
Segna di Buonaventura	14
Settignano (Desiderio di), *see* Desiderio.	
Signorelli (Luca)	52, 67, 84
Simone da Donatello	32, 38
Spinelli (Parri), *see* Parri.	
Spinello Aretino	11, 16-17, 21, 82
Taddeo di Bartolo	16
Taddeo Gaddi, *see* Gaddi.	
Tino	28
Tisi (Benvenuto), *see* Garofalo.	
Titian, *see* Tiziano.	
Tiziano Vecellio	87
Tommaso di Ser Giovanni, *see* Masaccio.	
Tommaso di Stefano, *see* Giottino.	
Traini, Francesco	21
Tura, Cosimo	90
Uccello, Paolo	41-43, 47, 48, 50, 53, 60, 72
Ugolino da Siena	15, 22
Vasari (Giorgio)	6, 46, 48, 52, 58, 59, 69, 86, 88
Veneziano (Antonio), *see* Antonio.	
Veneziano (Domenico), *see* Domenico.	
Ventura (Agnolo di), *see* Agnolo.	
Verrocchio, Andrea	44, 46-47, 53
Volterra, Francesco da	11, 20

PART I.

INDEX

OF

PLACES MENTIONED.

	Page
Arezzo - - - - - - -	12, 16, 17
,, church of S. Agostino - - - - -	16
,, cathedral of Arezzo - - - - -	16, 28
,, church of S. Francesco - - - -	49
Assisi - - - - - - - -	20
,, church of S. Francesco - - -	2, 3, 21, 82
Athens - - - - - - - -	1
Bergamo - - - - - - -	38
,, gallery of Bergamo - - - -	61
Berlin, gallery of Berlin - - - -	58, 65, 68, 69, 72
Bologna, shrine of S. Dominic - - - -	8, 9, 65
,, church of S. Petronius - - - -	29
Borgo San Sepolchro - - - - -	48
,, Compagnia della Misericordia - -	49
,, S. Giovanni Evangelista - - -	49
Byzantium, church of S. Sofia - - - -	1
Casole, near Siena - - - - -	28
Castiglione Fiorentino - - - - -	14
Castiglione di Olona - - - - -	50
Catacombs - - - - - - -	1
Certosa (of Pavia) - - - - -	38
,, (of the Val d'Ema) - - - -	34
Dresden Gallery - - - - -	67, 87
Empoli - - - - - - -	53
Fiesole, cathedral of Fiesole - - - -	36
,, convent of S. Domenico - - -	52, 54
Florence - - - - -	2, 12, 38, 40, 76
,, Accademia - 2, 13, 21, 47, 53, 58, 62, 65, 67, 70, 90
,, Badia - - - - - -	35
,, baptistery - - 2, 19, 27, 28, 29, 30, 33, 62
,, campanile of S. Maria del Fiore - - 5, 19, 29, 34
,, cathedral (S. Maria del Fiore) - - 5, 27, 28, 42, 60
,, church of S. Ambrogio - - - -	64

		Page
Florence, church of S^ma. Annunziata		62, 64
,, church of the Carmine (Brancacci chapel)	- 50, 51, 63, 66, 71,	82, 84
,, church of Santa Croce	- 3, 4, 18, 20, 36, 37, 48, 53, 75	
,, church of S. Lorenzo		62
,, church of S. Maria Novella	2, 19, 20, 22, 26, 37, 43, 64, 74	
,, church of S. Maria Maddalena dei Pazzi		64
,, church of S. Maria Nuova		48
,, church of S. Miniato		36, 42, 62
,, church of Ognissanti		71, 72
,, church of Or San Michele	- 21, 23, 31, 52, 46, 60	
,, church of S. Pietro Maggiori		22
,, church of Sta. Trinità		62, 73, 74
,, convent of the Carmine		57
,, convent of S. Marco		54, 73
,, Hospital of the Innocents		34
,, Mercatanzia		45
,, Monte Oliveto		53
,, Opera del Duomo		34
,, Palazzo Medici (now Riccardi)		31, 55
,, Palazzo Pitti, *see* Pitti.		
,, Palace of the Podesta or Bargello	- 4, 29, 31, 36, 44	
,, Palazzo Strozzi		37
,, Palazzo Vecchio		46, 62, 70, 73
,, Pitti Palace (and Gallery)		45, 60, 67
,, Sisterhood of S. Giorgio		61
,, Uffizi Gallery	- 3, 17, 20, 41, 45,!49, 52, 62, 64, 65, 66, 68, 69,	70, 90
,, villa of Caffagiolo		81
,, villa of Careggi		31, 46
Foggia		8
Genoa, Duomo		36
Gimignano, San		75
,, church of S. Agostino		37, 55
,, Capella di S. Fina		73, 75
,, Duomo		37
,, Oratory of S. Giovanni		73
,, Palazzo del Podestá		16
,, Pieve of S. Gimignano		75
Giovanni, San (upper Arno)		50
Gualfonda		41
Legnaia, Villa Pandolfini		47
London, Houses of Parliament		82
,, National Gallery	- 2, 14, 15, 17, 21, 22, 41, 45, 47, 48, 49, 55,	58, 61, 65, 67, 69, 72, 81, 87, 90
Lucca		12, 36
,, cathedral of Lucca		36
,, church of S. Martino		6, 7
Milan		2
,, Palazzo Vismara		32
Modena Cathedral		35
Montefalco		55
Montepulciano		32

	Page
Munich Gallery	65
Naples, Castel del Uovo	16
„ convent of Santa Chiara	4
„ L'Inconorata (built by Joanna I.)	4
„ Monte Oliveto of Naples	38
Orvieto, church of S. Corporale	16
„ church of S. Domenico	12, 15
„ Duomo of Orvieto	9, 12, 20, 22, 28, 55
Padua	31
„ church of St. Antonio	4, 47
„ church of S. Maria dell' Arena	3, 4, 82
„ Eremitani Chapel	59, 82
Paris, Hotel Cluny	53
„ Louvre Gallery	41, 54, 61, 75, 90
Perugia, church of S. Domenico	11
„ church of S. Pietro Cassinense	35
„ fountain of Perugia	8, 10
„ Oratory of S. Bernardino	35
„ Sala del Cambio	73
Pisa	2, 8, 76
„ baptistery of Pisa	7, 10
„ Campo Santo of Pisa	2, 6, 10, 11, 12, 14, 17, 20, 21, 22, 23–26, 55, 82
„ cathedral of Pisa	11
„ chapterhouse of S. Bonaventura	16
„ convent of S. Catherine	9, 15
„ church of S. Francesco	16, 18
„ church of S. Maria della Spina	20
Pistoja, church of S. Andrea	10
„ church of S. Francesco al Prato	20
„ church of S. Giovanni Fuorcivitas	9
„ Ospedale del Ceppo	34
Prato	16, 34, 65, 82
„ cathedral of Prato	35, 59
„ convent chapel of S. Margherita	52, 54, 59, 60, 63
„ church of S. Donato al Scopeto	65
Ravello	8
Ravenna, church of S. Apollinare Nuovo	1
„ church of S. Maria in Cosmedin	1
„ church of S. Michele in Affricisco	1
Rimini	27
„ temple of S. Francesco	32, 38
Rome, basilica of S. Giovanni Laterano	4
„ cathedral of S. Peter	32
„ church of S. Clemente	50, 51
„ church of S. Lorenzo fuori le Mura	1
„ church of S. Maria sopra Minerva	55, 64
„ church of S. Pudentiana	1
„ church of S. Teodoro	1
„ Navicella (mosaic)	4
„ Vatican	55, 87
„ Capella Sistina of Vatican	64, 66, 67, 73, 75, 82
„ Stanze of the Vatican	82

San Gimignano, see Gimignano (S.).
San Giovanni, see Giovanni (S.).

	Page
Sieña	12, 28, 76
,, cathedral of Sieña	7, 13, 28
,, church of S. Agostino	16, 17
,, church of S. Domenico	12, 17
,, Fonte Gaia	28
,, Gallery of Sieña	12, 17, 21
,, Libreria of Duomo	82
,, Palazzo Pubblico	14, 15, 16, 82
,, Sala dei Novi e della Pace	14
,, Sala di Balia	17
Spoleto	62, 82
,, cathedral of Spoleto	62, 63, 64
Tuscany	1, 34, 38, 63
Urbino Palace	38, 42
Vallombrosa	75
Varallo (Sacro Monte)	38
Venice, cathedral of S. Marco	1, 32
,, Scuola of S. Marco	47
,, tombs of the Doges	38
Verona, tombs of the Scaligers	38

www.ingramcontent.com/pod-product-compliance
Lightning Source LLC
Chambersburg PA
CBHW022137160426
43197CB00009B/1322